I0949798

NIGHT CALL

Robert Wicks, a renowned psychologist and specialist in the area of resilience, has written a truly impressive book. In sharing experiences from his own personal and professional life, he has provided remarkable insights about taking care of others while making certain we also engage in self-compassion and self-care in order to avoid disillusionment and burnout. Robert's openness, empathy, and wisdom are apparent on each page as he highlights realistic principles for living a purposeful and meaningful life—a life in which we touch the hearts and souls of others while recognizing the importance of maintaining our own balance and resilience. This is one of those rare works that can serve as a wonderful resource for anyone who has the responsibility for caring for another person while at the same time being relevant for those of us in the helping and healing professions.

ROBERT BROOKS, PHD
FACULTY, HARVARD MEDICAL SCHOOL
CO-AUTHOR OF *The Power of Resilience*

Night Call provides an important wake-up call for those of us in healthcare. Robert Wicks raises our awareness of the importance of tending to our inner peace and resiliency as he states "you can't share what you don't have." The book identifies the need for finding a reflective space and alone time and guides us how to "lean back and reflect." Caring is core to the practice discipline of nursing, and this book reminds us that in order to maintain a compassionate presence with our patients and families, we must take the time to care for ourselves. For nurses in academia, the tripart mission of clinical practice, teaching, and research can be incredibly synergistic and rewarding yet challenging and exhausting at times. Dr. Wicks gives us tips on how to mentally manage our work, maintain a healthy perspective between work and family, and identify the value of mentors throughout our careers.

M. TISH KNOBF, PHD, RN, FAAN
PROFESSOR
YALE UNIVERSITY SCHOOL OF NURSING

Robert Wicks not only makes me look at my inner self—my goals, my positive and negative thoughts about my work, but also how I can value and learn from the "negative." This book gently and comprehensively leads those reaching out to others in their circle of family and friends, as well as healing and helping professionals, to a heightened sensitivity to the needs of the people they serve—in my case, the ill, dying persons, their caregivers, and the bereaved.

J. Shep Jeffreys, EdD, Fellow in Thanatology

Psychiatry Faculty

Johns Hopkins School of Medicine

Author, *Helping Grieving People: When Tears Are Not Enough*

Night Call by Robert Wicks helps caregivers to slow down, to pay as much attention to themselves and their own needs as they do the needs of those they are serving. Many books will advocate for self-care, but Dr. Wicks shows you how to do it. The conversational tone and lack of psychological jargon can be deceptive. The book is easy to read but filled with seasoned wisdom. A splendid book not only for health-caregivers but also for clergy, family caregivers, and anyone whose focus is on serving the lives of those they love.

Deborah van Dusen Hunsinger, PhD

Charles W. Newcombe Professor of Pastoral Theology

Princeton Theological Seminary

Professional counselors and psychologists will enjoy this profound and thoughtful exposition of resilience. The author has been a leading figure for years in this area, but now we are realizing that building resilience is what counseling and therapy are about. The writing is clear, with many fascinating case examples, which will help us all in clinical and counseling practice. The book discusses what we are about—building client health. Solving problems is a beginning, but our real goal is resilience. I recommend this book highly.

Allen E. Ivey, EdD, ABPP

Board Certified in Counseling Psychology

Distinguished University Professor (Emeritus)

University of Massachusetts, Amherst

[*Night Call*] is an inspiring book filled with life lessons and practice wisdom that will be of value to all practitioners. Through well-documented stories and anecdotes, Wicks has communicated the importance of patience, persistence, and compassion in the helping process. The book ends with a call to evaluate the next steps in personal growth. I highly recommend this book . . . it is a wonderful read that will inspire and sustain you through the darkest of nights.

CYNTHIA FRANKLIN, PhD, LCSW, LMFT
ASSOCIATE DEAN FOR DOCTORAL EDUCATION AND STIERNBERG/
SPENCER FAMILY PROFESSOR IN MENTAL HEALTH
THE UNIVERSITY OF TEXAS AT AUSTIN SCHOOL OF
SOCIAL WORK

Night Call is a valuable guide for people who wonder how to help those who suffer and for people worn down by the seemingly endless sickness of those they care for. With stories and words of wisdom, Wicks shows how persistence, compassion, and humility heal us all. His book is a great salve.

ROBERT F. KENNEDY, JR.

The Resilient Clinician (Oxford University Press)

"As therapists we need to stop and reflect, be aware of our negative emotions, get new perspectives, learn to self-care, and know how to untie the knots of our inner life. Robert Wicks has written an engaging book reminding us of this."

STEPHEN JOSEPH, PhD
AUTHOR, *What Doesn't Kill Us: A New Psychology of Posttraumatic Growth*
PROFESSOR, CENTER FOR TRAUMA, RESILIENCE AND GROWTH
UNIVERSITY OF NOTTINGHAM (UK)

Overcoming Secondary Stress in Medical and Nursing Practice (Oxford University Press)

"This power-packed book is a must-read for all professionals who are responsible for the healthcare of others."

RUTH McCORKLE, PhD, FAAN
THE FLORENCE S. WALD PROFESSOR OF NURSING
YALE UNIVERSITY SCHOOL OF NURSING

Primer on Posttraumatic Growth with Mary Beth Werdel (Wiley)

"This book is an important and integrative addition to the literature on posttraumatic growth."

CHRISTINE A. COURTOIS, PhD, ABPP
AUTHOR, *Healing the Incest Wound: Adult Survivors in Therapy*
(REVISED EDITION)

NIGHT CALL

EMBRACING COMPASSION AND HOPE IN
A TROUBLED WORLD

ROBERT J. WICKS

Author of
Perspective: The Calm within the Storm
and
The Resilient Clinician

*~ Share in the "quiet lessons" that helping and healing professionals
are taught on discovering new strength within life's whirlwinds. ~*

OXFORD
UNIVERSITY PRESS

OXFORD
UNIVERSITY PRESS

Oxford University Press is a department of the University of Oxford. It furthers
the University's objective of excellence in research, scholarship, and education
by publishing worldwide. Oxford is a registered trade mark of Oxford University
Press in the UK and certain other countries.

Published in the United States of America by Oxford University Press
198 Madison Avenue, New York, NY 10016, United States of America.

Library of Congress Cataloging-in-Publication Data
Names: Wicks, Robert J., author.
Title: Night call : embracing compassion and hope in a troubled world / by Robert J. Wicks.
Description: New York, NY : Oxford University Press, [2018] |
Includes bibliographical references and index.
Identifiers: LCCN 2017017852 (print) | LCCN 2017000502 (ebook) |
ISBN 9780190669638 (alk. paper) | ISBN 9780190884031 (custom hardcover)
Subjects: LCSH: Resilience (Personality trait) | Compassion. | Counseling. |
Social service. | Human services.
Classification: LCC BF698.35.R47 W543 2018 (ebook) |
LCC BF698.35.R47 (print) | DDC 155.2/4—dc23
LC record available at https://lccn.loc.gov/2017017852

1 3 5 7 9 8 6 4 2

Printed by Sheridan Books, Inc., United States of America

The author would like to express his gratitude to the following publishers for permission to
use or adapt material from the following publications:

Wicks, Robert J. *The Inner Life of the Counselor.* (Hoboken, NJ: Wiley) Copyright © 2012 by
John Wiley & Sons.

Excerpts and adapted text from the following titles are used by permission Ave Maria Press/
Sorin Books, all rights reserved: *Crossing the Desert*, copyright © 2000 by Robert J. Wicks; *No
Problem*, copyright © 2014 by Robert J. Wicks; *Riding the Dragon*, copyright © 2012 by Robert
J. Wicks; *Simple Changes*, copyright © 2006 by Robert J. Wicks; *Streams of Contentment*, copyright
© 2013 by Robert J. Wicks; *Touching the Holy*, 2007 copyright © by Robert J. Wicks.

Excerpts and adapted text from the following titles are used by permission Paulist Press,
all rights reserved: *Living a Gentle, Passionate Life*, copyright © 1998 by Robert J. Wicks;
Living Simply in an Anxious World, copyright © 1988 by Robert J. Wicks; *After 50*,
copyright © 1997 by Robert J. Wicks.

For three women of valor and commitment to what is good
in this world . . .
My mother, Mae Wicks
My wife, Michaele Barry Wicks
and
My daughter, Michaele Wicks Kulick

When I read the following words of David Brooks, I think of you:

The people we admire for being resilient are not hard; they are ardent . . . They have a fervent commitment to some cause, some ideal or relationship. That higher yearning enables them to withstand setbacks, pain and betrayal. . . . We are all fragile when we don't know what our purpose is, when we haven't thrown ourselves with abandon into a social role, when we haven't committed ourselves to certain people, when we feel like a swimmer in an ocean with no edge. . . . People are really tough only after they have taken a leap of faith for some truth or mission or love. Once they've done that they can withstand a lot. We live in an age when it's considered sophisticated to be disenchanted. But people who are enchanted are the real tough cookies.

New York Times (August 30, 2016)

I don't know what your destiny will be
but one thing I do know.
The only ones among you who will be really happy
are those who have sought and found how to serve.
~ ALBERT SCHWEITZER

Do not believe that he who seeks to comfort you lives untroubled
among the simple and quiet words that sometimes do you good.
His life has much difficulty and sadness and remains far behind
yours. Were it otherwise he would never have been able to find
those words.
~ RAINER MARIA RILKE
Letters to a Young Poet

CONTENTS

Resiliency psychology: The process of not only assisting people to bounce back from adversity but also setting the stage for them, as well as the helpers themselves, to become deeper persons as a result of the very challenges they are facing.

HEARING THE WHISPERS OF A RESILIENT, COMPASSIONATE LIFE: A PROLOGUE

You don't have to sit outside in the dark.
If, however, you wish to look at the stars,
you will find the darkness is necessary.
—ANNIE DILLARD, *Teaching a Stone to Talk*

During a presentation to ministers, a lecturer asked an intended rhetorical question, "What do you think is the core of your work?" But before he could proceed, surprisingly, one of the clerics in the audience yelled out, "Helping people through the night." The same can also be said of physicians, nurses, psychologists, social workers, counselors, relief and nongovernmental organization workers, educators, others in the helping and healing professions, and really any of us who take on a caring role.

For more than 30 years, the primary focus of my work has been to supervise, mentor, teach, and treat persons in these professional roles. As they walked with others in the darkness, I journeyed with them—especially when as professionals they became lost, discouraged, disillusioned, or traumatized because of the work in which they were involved (what is now called "*secondary* stress").

As well as individual work with these helpers, much of my efforts also involved delivering presentations to varied groups of caregivers on resilience, self-care, and on how to maintain a healthy perspective. I also often addressed the general public because all of us are required to be caregivers of some type at different times in our lives.

In the United States I was privileged to speak at such venues as Walter Reed Army Hospital and at a commemoration of the 2013 Boston marathon bombing, as well as in such areas abroad as Beirut, Phnom Penh, Belfast, Guatemala City, Haiti, Cape Town, Budapest, Hanoi, and in other places where caregivers were experiencing great professional stress and personal anxiety. In these settings, I was impressed not only by the challenges these helpers and healers were facing but even more so by their openness, humility, and willingness to let go when the percept they were holding onto, which was causing them so much pain, was challenged.

For instance, after a presentation in South Africa to those involved in caring for the poor, a social worker raised her hand to get my attention. When I asked her if she had a question, she exclaimed, "I can't do it anymore. I need to leave the profession . . . *now!*"

"What exactly is the nature of your work?" I asked.

She responded, "I help women who have been raped or abused. They are poor and usually single parents. When I go with them to court, they must take a day off from work, which they can ill afford. Then when we get there, the judge—who is usually male—often looks at the papers we hand him, shrugs, makes a face, and says, 'I haven't had time to look over the case yet. Make another appointment.' It is just so discouraging. What I do is useless. *I* am useless."

I let the emotion in the moment settle for a time. Then, after a period of quiet, I said to her, "Given what you have told me, I have a few questions for you. First, who else was with this woman during her time of desolation?"

"Only me."

"Would it be an overstatement to say at that moment you were emotionally closer to her than anyone else in the world?"

She paused for a moment and answered in a hoarse voice, "No it wouldn't be. She had only me. There was no one else."

In response, I looked at her, and in as gentle a voice as I could muster, asked, "And you want to leave that?" Then, after another period of quiet tearfulness on her part, I added, "We all make the mistake of focusing solely on apparent success. But, it is not success that matters. It is personal and professional *faithfulness*. We should never underestimate the power of that even though the world might tell us it is only immediate desired results that matter."

Not only helpers need to hear this, everyone does. Parents often feel lost when their children go astray even though they have done their best to help them traverse the psychological deserts of life that young people must face and cross as part of growing up. In marriages, spouses often lose their way when marital problems come up and seem to overwhelm them.

When the workplace turns toxic for any of us, the lessons that all caregivers must learn if they are to remain vital are also relevant to all of our situations.

What professional helpers and healers learn at some point if they want to continue to remain as faithful guides is that how they view their care for others, especially when it is most challenging, is a crucial factor. As I have mentioned in three previous books (*Bounce: Living the Resilient Life*; *Perspective: The Calm within the Storm*; and *Riding the Dragon: 10 Lessons for Inner Strength in Challenging Times*), self-care, maintaining a healthy perspective, learning approaches to expanding one's resiliency range, and understanding the importance of self-renewal all help in this regard. However, beyond this, there are wonderful simple, powerful lessons worth being appreciated anew by all of us on how to enjoy a more rewarding life. In this regard, I have found that even in some of the passing encounters experienced in the work I do, there have been "whispers" of a meaningful way to approach our brief time on this earth. I believe they are worth sharing here so all of us—no matter what our role in life is—can appreciate them.

In *Night Call*, the results of this search for what can provide and strengthen such an attitude toward all of life are offered in the form of "quiet lessons." They are purposely brief given the fast pace and busy schedules of most people in today's stressful world. To be honest, they are not designed to be a "quick fix." Putting them into practice will take both reflection and perseverance. As Annie Dillard aptly remarks in her book, *The Writing Life*, "There is no shortage of good days. It is good lives that are hard to come by." Yes, she's right . . . but it is all worth the right type of efforts to make it so.

REVISITING THE "QUIET LESSONS"

In my work I have always had two fairly simple goals: to enable people to enjoy their lives a little more and to help them better appreciate the amazing breakthroughs possible when they can stand in the darkness with a new sense of openness. When this happens, they will benefit and also be in a position to be a beacon of hope for others. As Matthieu Ricard aptly notes in his book, *Happiness*, "Everything changed when I met a few remarkable human beings who exemplified what a fulfilling human life can be." When you meet people like this, you can even see it in their smiles, their authentic appreciation of the short time they have left on this earth, as well as in their ability to reach out to their family, friends, and those who come to them for support, encouragement, and the fostering of possible new insights.

When I have been able to aid helping professionals and others in need to realize that rejection, small rebuffs, great failures, misfortune, and even trauma are *not* the last word, life became something new, dear, and precious to them in so many—often new—ways. The sadness for the loss or the negative events they encountered didn't disappear of course. Those events certainly weren't seen as anything desirable. However, breakthroughs in mentoring, coaching, or therapy are often marked by a recognition that with openness and gentleness we may experience growth, depth, and an ability to be compassionate in ways that could not have been possible had the terrible events not happened in the first place.

It is not *if* terrible things will confront us, but *when*. Thus, our perspective can destroy or grow us. True sadness can become growth-filled so that we can embrace amazing new experiences and wisdom. However, to accomplish this, we must also become newly attuned to lessons that society at large sadly often ignores, ridicules, or dismisses.

Psychology, philosophy, and classic spirituality, for the most part, are at their best when they are countercultural. Most recently, positive psychology went against the tendency of many helpers, guides, and society to focus more on the problems people have than on the possibly unexplored gifts they possess. Positive psychologists asked, "Why isn't the positive news about ourselves just as important—in some cases, even *more* important—than the negative aspects?" (We can also ask this today of our news media, which reports troubling events in a way that positive efforts, actions, and results seem unimportant or "fluff" in terms of what is worth uncovering, attending to, or reporting.)

Narrative therapy paralleled the positive psychology movement by also emphasizing that persons must be seen as having the copyright on their own stories. Accordingly, persons from this school of thought believe everyone should be involved in being assertive in ensuring that family and society mores don't dictate or limit their own self-definition in ways that are obvious (conscious) or hidden (unconscious).

In a similar vein, in this book the "lessons" (or what some may term as "signature strengths" or "virtues") on such themes as ordinariness, acceptance, and forgiveness—in a world that often tries to convince us otherwise—will be discussed. At times, it certainly will be going against the current tide of what is fashionably termed as "good." A major goal in offering such lessons is to help people return to the intensity and confusion of life a little differently, more gently, with a clearer eye, and a greater sense of compassion for themselves and those around them who may be presently embroiled in confusion and experiencing anxiety because of it.

The list of lessons and themes to be presented in the chapters and appendix are based on insights gleaned from both the lives and writings of a number of critical thinkers from psychology, classic spirituality, literature, and other areas, as well as my own clinical work with, and mentoring of, persons in the healing and helping professions. One of my hopes in offering these topics is that they will spur a *reconsideration* of how to best emulate the psychological virtues they exemplify in more intentional, possibly more vital ways. However, in offering them, there is also an implicit invitation to round out the list by inspiring people to create or adapt additional themes that seem more personally pertinent. In doing this, the process of raising one's own further attunement to the lessons of life's heretofore "quiet lessons" can improve. Accordingly such personal involvement would also increase the possibility— as the result of one's own initiative—that they will be lived out in new ways rather than merely considered as perennial possibilities.

In line with this, perhaps a more efficacious way to initially get pulled into the thrust of the philosophy of this book is to look through the table of contents, choose a topic that especially strikes you, and start there rather than at the beginning. Once you do this and read about that lesson or virtue, my suggestion is to then put the book down and reflect for a few moments on what it might mean in terms of your own life. This should lead to determining what practice, change, or new sensitivity can be incorporated into your own outlook. It will also help to jumpstart the motivation to go further so a sense of intrigue about how you are currently both viewing and leading life at this point can be expanded. Such knowledge can then provide the basis of additional information leading to new, possibly greater, wisdom and more fulfilling actions in how you both view and live this brief life we have been given.

In this spirit, by drawing upon the findings and comments of contemporary psychological and classic spiritual wisdom figures as well as my own clinical experience, the following chapters are meant to be like a series of teachings from a mentor sitting across from you with whom you are meeting as a way of enhancing the experience of your own life. How the lessons are adopted and incorporated will be up to you. Only you can decide how far you want to involve yourself in this pursuit.

As you consider this, a reality that must be put out front is that each lesson, theme, or virtue is not like a vitamin pill to be swallowed, followed by a waiting period to see if and how it will work. Instead, it is like turning the page and finding a recipe that must be examined closely, altered to your individual taste, and carefully prepared so it is a psychological meal that nourishes you in a way that "the dining experience" (process of gaining new insight) is most likely to be repeated again and again. Such desire is so important because practice and failure will be at the forefront of finding and instilling the quiet lessons more clearly and deeply in your outlook and way of life. It is not how often one fails that is at issue. The issue is how much can be learned from each failure in an effort to remain faithful to the process of enriching the music of one's life by revisiting values or virtues that may have been broached or are from childhood, but for some reason, may have lost their luster in adulthood.

In doing this, it may be possible to find that

> *ordinariness* is not dull and a failure to be unique. It is being free from allowing others to dictate what you need to be happy and significant.

acceptance is not tantamount to resignation. It is seeing life clearly as it is, not as we would have it to be, so we can make the most of it.

forgiveness is not capitulating. It is letting go of the chains of past hurts so we don't remain imprisoned because of others' or our own past bad behaviors.

Hearing the whispers of a rewarding life by revisiting quiet lessons society may have set aside or derided is an essential step in leading a meaningful and fulfilling life—no matter what is going on around and within you. It is like slowly finding the next part of yourself as you experience the present and move into the future. Professional helpers and healers have had to learn this, sometimes the hard way, in order to launch and continue their healing mission and relish their own lives. In today's anxious, stressful world, it would benefit *all* of us to learn such quiet lessons and practice them as well. One's quality of life going forward may well depend on it. In addition, the quality of our presence and availability to others may be affected in turn. As the famous Chinese proverb goes, "When the tide rises, the boats in the water do as well."

Often we fail to realize this, and not only do we lose out but others do as well. This comes across clearly in a beautiful story told by Edwina Gateley, who works with homeless and abused women. It goes something like this:

Once upon a time there was a country ruled by a king. The country was invaded and the king was killed, but his children were rescued by servants and hidden away. The smallest, an infant daughter, was reared by a peasant family. They didn't know she was the king's daughter. She had become the peasant's daughter and she dug potatoes and lived in poverty.

One day an old woman came out of the forest and approached the young woman who was digging potatoes. The old woman asked her, "Do you know who you are?" And the young woman said, "Yes, I'm the peasant's daughter and a potato digger." The old woman said, "No, no, you are the daughter of the king." And the potato digger said, *"I'm the daughter of the king?"* "Yes, yes, that's who you are!" she replied and then disappeared back into the forest.

After the old woman left, the young woman still dug potatoes but she dug them differently. It was the way she held her shoulders and it was the light in her eyes because she knew who she really was. She knew she was the daughter of the king.

The key message this story conveys is one of empowerment. Through it we are called to help people see who they are—especially when they are experiencing personal darkness. We must go from place to place and through our presence ask others metaphorically, "Do you know who you are?" However, to accomplish this, we must also take the time and effort to know who we truly are, what our gifts might be, and how we can share them in a way that we can reach out without being pulled down.

This book will only justify itself if it can help people realize more clearly the delight of their lives and help them walk with others during tough times. Material on "resiliency psychology," which has been developed for living and standing with others in an anxious world, is now within our reach. The very information given to helping and healing professionals is now available to all of us, and given the demands on people today to be better parents, siblings, caretakers, coworkers, and friends, this wisdom is worth mining. Hearing the whispers of a rewarding life deserves the effort.

Vladimir Horowitz once quipped, "The piano is the easiest instrument to play but the hardest instrument to play well." I think the same can be said of leading a meaningful life that includes, of course, being compassionate. Most people can and do reach out a helping hand to others at times. However, reaching out without being pulled down as a way of life is a totally different way of being, which is *both* possible and difficult if we make the effort to remain resilient. Yet once again, the pressing question remains, "Will we take the time and expend the energy to do so?"

Night Call

THE QUIET LESSONS

ONE

"Come Sit by Me"

They may forget what you said but they
will never forget how you made them feel.
—Carl Buehner

In 2001, I was asked to work for a second time with English-speaking helpers in Cambodia who were there to help the Khmer people rebuild their nation after years of terror and torture. I had been there before in 1996 as they prepared for their first elections after the Vietnamese invaded and pushed the Khmer Rouge into the northern part of the country. This second visit came about because of an offhand comment I made upon leaving the first time, saying I would come back again if they needed me. At the time, I was merely trying to be nice, not thinking they would ever take me up on it. I was wrong. One of the organizers remembered what I had said and told the person who was responsible for originally bringing me there, "He said he would come back if we needed him and he wouldn't lie, would he?" So here I was once again.

In this visit, the audience was much more varied. Hindu psychiatrists sat in one corner, American Buddhist aid workers in another, Mother Teresa's nuns were present, and there were also many professionals from international secular relief organizations. In addition, at least half of them spoke English only as a second language. I was also informed that most of them had not taken off two days in a row—the length of the conference—for more than a year. And so if they didn't feel it was worthwhile at the time for the first breakout group, they would simply get up, leave, and not return.

From what I could sense, the workshop was going fairly well thus far. However, after the first day, I was still feeling the stress of performance anxiety. And so as I suggest to others experiencing stress, I decided to take a walk, in this case, along the Mekong River. I also toured the main Buddhist temple whose walls were still pockmarked with bullet holes. As I was doing this, I heard a noise and looked up only to see that the skies had suddenly darkened in preparation for the brief but drenching storms that would move through the area at this time of year.

As I was thinking about where to seek shelter, it began to rain, lightly at first, but then quite heavily. I was caught out in the open and thought, "Ah, well" when I saw in the distance a Khmer shopkeeper waving me over to take shelter with him. In response, I ran over to his "establishment," which really was a stall consisting of just a couple of tables of goods with an overhang that shielded shoppers from the bright sun or, in this case, the heavy rain.

By the time I got to him, even though it was a brief sprint, the rains were really coming down. As I approached, I saw him pat a section of the table with his left hand and smile at me broadly as if to nonverbally say, "Come sit by me." In return, I nodded my head because I knew only a few words of Khmer, and he, as I would discover, knew some French but no English. We sat together quietly. He didn't seem concerned about his loss of business because of the weather, and I was in no hurry to go anywhere else. During the remainder of the few hours break I had only planned a visit to a small museum on my list of places to see.

The rain was gone in about twenty minutes but the positive results of the experience were surprisingly amazing. Sitting there thinking about the man's spontaneous compassion, his ease at taking an unexpected break in his work, and his appreciation of my smile and expression of gratitude as I joined together the tips of my hands and gestured toward him when I got up to leave, made me appreciate a positive undercurrent of simplicity in his life and our interaction.

While walking away, I thought to myself, I want to possess more deeply that type of simple graciousness the shopkeeper gave to someone he did not know and who could not do anything for him. I wanted this attitude even though I knew that it was so often scorned by a society that keeps score on what is given out in order to ensure that it is returned in measure or with interest. While many multimillionaires would respond with scorn to the idea that their Social Security payments be lessened so the poor could have more, this man with so little shared what he had with me. Moreover, he didn't do it out of guilt or duty, but because it was the natural thing for him to do at that time. Giving and expecting nothing in return is true graciousness, and it seemed to make him happy too! I wanted that attitude, so I kept the experience midbrain in the hopes that I could understand it more fully. But, as I was to find out, giving of yourself takes opening yourself up and recognizing when egoism plays interference with receiving and accepting life as it is.

Once I was treating an adult patient who as a child had been sexually abused by a close relative. After a fairly long stretch of weekly therapy, we were coming to the end of the treatment. She was quite animated as she was telling me a story about an interaction she had earlier in the day. Her focus had long ceased being primarily on the past and was now more present and future oriented, which was a sign of the significant progress she had made. Noticing this, I wanted to make an intervention by offering a question. However, I wanted to think through my goals first by asking myself the same four questions I ask of clinicians I supervise when they say something to a patient or client:

Why did you say that?
Why did you say that *now*?

Why did you say that now *in that way?*

And as the caregiver, what did you expect?

In response to this thinking, I realized I wanted to say something that would help this patient recognize and honor the hard work she had undertaken in therapy. Also, it was my goal to ask her how she had arrived at this point so when she entered darkness again—for darkness comes and goes for us all—she would know what to do. At least that was my hope.

However, like many therapists with a plan, I was in for a surprise when I finally formulated in my mind the phrase and asked, "Picture my face as a mirror. What do you see?"

"Oh, I see a woman alive with a great spirit. She has integrated the little child that was lost with the woman she is now and because of it she is *hot stuff!*"

I had to laugh in response to her newfound exuberance and more accurate appreciation of the wonderful person she always really was and is. I then added, "Well how did you get to this point? You certainly weren't this way when you first came in to see me."

She looked back at me, made a face, and said, "You mean you don't know?"

I said, "Not exactly. I would never ask you a question to which I knew the full answer."

"Well, it was quite simple."

"*Simple?*" I responded, quite curious about what she was going to say next.

"Yes. The first time I came in to see you, I simply watched how you sat with me, and then I began sitting with myself in the same way."

These words brought me back to what a counseling student of mine, who also played the organ at church, shared with me:

At a funeral, a small somewhat scrawny little boy came upstairs to the music loft to see me after the funeral service. For him to come upstairs alone was a little odd since children usually do not wander around at a funeral. I asked him if he knew where his parents were. He told me very matter-of-factly, "Well, my mommy is downstairs; she said I could come up to see you. But my daddy is down there now" (pointing to the casket downstairs).

Unbeknownst to me, since I was not introduced to the family of the funeral party, the boy was the son of the man who had just died. I immediately crunched down on my teeth, held my breath, and willed myself not to cry since I was sure this boy had already seen enough tears. But I couldn't help but wonder to myself, What in the world was his mother thinking to send him up here?! And I just said, "Oh."

As a counseling student, I am sure there was something much better to say to a seven-year-old boy who had just lost his father, but as it turned out, that one word was sufficient. It reassured him and gave him enough confidence to tell me, "That song about eagle's wings was my daddy's favorite song and he sung it real loud at church. Now it's my favorite song too!"

I couldn't say anything because I had rocks in my throat. He then went over to the balcony and looked down below at the casket sitting in the aisle with the beautiful white lace cover over it. He turned around, looked at me briefly, touched the organ keys very quickly, and ran down the stairs. I tried to say goodbye but nothing came out.

Several minutes later, the widow came upstairs apologizing for her son's intrusion and I reassured her that it was no problem. She then proceeded to tell me that he had not spoken one word or cried or eaten solid food since his dad had died. And she thanked me for my playing the song "On Eagle's Wings" because it opened him up.

His name, as I learned later, was Davie, David Jr. for his dad, and all I will ever know about him is that his favorite song is "On Eagle's Wings" by Michael Joncas.

Both of these women brought me back, at that moment, to a recollection from early in my clinical practice on how profound an impact presence and respect for another human being can be—no matter what role we may be playing in the person's life. It was during a very intense period of my life immediately after receiving my doctorate in psychology from Hahnemann Medical College and Hospital. At the time, I was on the faculty of the Graduate School of Social Work and Social Research at Bryn Mawr College; had a clinical practice in Center City,

Philadelphia; and was also on the professional staff of a hospital in Lancaster, Pennsylvania, where I would make rounds for the director of psychiatry on Sundays.

Driving down the Lincoln Highway on a sunny Sunday morning to make rounds at the hospital was normally a joy for me. In addition to patients on the psychiatric service, there were some medical patients in intensive care or on other floors for whom we were providing consultant services. I enjoyed the work a great deal. Moreover, the ride was usually relaxing because it was through the picturesque Pennsylvania Dutch Country. The particular morning of the event in question, however, was different.

I had risen early, thinking I didn't have duty that day. I had just started to drink a cup of coffee and was reading the Sunday *New York Times* in the den when the phone rang. It was the head of psychiatry, and he wanted to know whether I planned to go to the hospital to provide coverage this morning. (I heard some tension in his voice as he said this.) I told him that he hadn't mentioned it when we had office hours early this week, so I thought I was off. Then he told me in fairly colorful language (that wasn't psychiatric in nature) what he thought about my interpretation, summarily told me to get out there, and abruptly hung up.

After this jolt to my relaxing morning plans, I thought, "Well, maybe I can quickly get in and out and be back home with my coffee and the paper in a couple of hours." I encountered the first block to this short-lived fantasy toward the end of the drive to the hospital. As I was moving rather quickly down the highway, I spotted the dreaded orange triangle. This is the bright symbol affixed to the back of Amish buggies to warn drivers behind them that they were moving slowly. *Very, very* slowly.

To make it worse, the buggy didn't turn off until we had practically reached the hospital. Finally, I pulled into the doctor's parking lot, double-stepped it up the stairs, and headed for the unit to see how many patients I would see. After nodding to the nurse at the station, I reviewed the list and saw there were only three names on it. Immediately, I smiled broadly and thought to myself, "Yes! This is going to be an early day."

At the start of my rounds, I visited a young Amish boy who had been in an accident. He looked a bit frightened, and I wound up doing most of the talking during the session, which normally isn't the case. Keeping a relaxed look, I sat down, leaned back, and chatted as if I had all day, in the hope of putting him at ease with me and his traumatic situation. After being there a while and noticing he was finally looking less anxious, I stood up and said, "I'll stop back again to see you before I leave," and I smiled. He looked up and said, "OK." My thought was as I left him, "Poor little fellow. He's still scared from the sudden, unexpected impact of a car hitting his buggy from behind."

When I moved on to see the other patients, thoughts of the young boy then faded from my mind. I had to be totally present to others in trouble. As a matter of fact, our encounter had slipped so much from my mind that when I finished the last patient visit, I went out to my car, forgetting my promise to return before leaving. Suddenly, just as I was getting in the car to leave, I remembered him. In response, my first thought was, "He probably won't remember and didn't get much out of our original contact anyway, so I can simply skip it and go home to my waiting newspaper and a hot cup of coffee." Then after a few seconds of vacillation as to what I should do, knowing myself as I do, I knew this would never work for me. So I slowly closed and locked the driver's door and went back into the hospital.

When I re-entered his room, I said cheerfully, "Well, I bet you thought I had forgotten you." In response, he looked up, smiled at the recognition of a now-familiar face in this strange environment for him, and said, "No, I *knew* you'd come back." His comment and the small pained smile on his face made me appreciate more deeply how we often don't see our effect on other people and the potential joy present in even brief, passing encounters with people who were previously strangers to us.

This little epiphany was something important to remember; it was both simple and profound. I could let it go as a nice but fleeting experience of meeting someone in need, or I could see it as a beacon shining on such temporary encounters with others. It demonstrated to me, early on, how important these moments of faithful presence on my part could be if only I recognized and appreciated their deep value—even if the results did not seem immediate or great.

Moreover, I believe this is not only the case in those instances where others in our family, circle of friends, associates, or new acquaintances come to us for help or feedback; it is just as significant in how we sit with *ourselves*. In a TV interview not long before he died, noted rabbi Abraham Joshua Heschel advised young people to build their lives as if they were works of art. To accomplish this, however, we must know *how* to explore both our own gifts as well as our growing edges (those areas that need improvement).

Too often we look at ourselves too harshly or defensively and this leads to either no new insight or a distorted self-knowledge. The three major blind alleys I have found in efforts at self-awareness are *arrogance*, in which we project the blame (and unfortunately simultaneously the power to change) onto others; *ignorance*, where we condemn ourselves (which leads nowhere because behavior that we wince at will eventually turn into behavior that we wink at); and *discouragement* (because we want immediate change).

The framework for self-respect is to view oneself with a sense of *intrigue* and to avoid being judgmental or defensive when viewing ourselves. Instead, with a balance of clarity and kindness, we seek to find our gifts, explore in what situations we psychologically trip over them, and look for ways we can alter our cognitions (ways of thinking, perceiving, and understanding situations, others, and ourselves) and behavior. The goal is to seek a greater sense of openness to new knowledge that will help us enjoy our own lives and gifts more fully so as to be able to share them with others more freely. It is a continual process of self-exploration that all of us have an opportunity to go through—even at those times when slight emotional disturbances wake us up to the opportunity to learn about ourselves.

For instance, a number of months ago I was walking through the neighborhood where I had recently bought a new townhome. I found the people living there were for the most part quite friendly and welcoming. As I was to find out during one of my walks, however, there is always the exception.

I had just turned onto my street on the way back to the house when I saw one of the residents in the distance. She was standing there with what appeared to be her grandchild. She looked at me briefly and I was ready to wave as was my custom and is that of most of the others who live here. However, she turned away so quickly that I put my hand down before it was fully up. I didn't think too much about it until I got closer and her daughter came out of the house and walked by me without even acknowledging my presence. The incident was so rare in our neighborhood that rather than brushing it off, I found myself personalizing the event. I could tell it had affected me by the type of exaggerated negative thoughts that were running through my head: "They saw me but ignored me either because they didn't know me or because they felt I wasn't of any use to them. They didn't even bother to stop, smile, and greet me. I was just another older person walking through the neighborhood who was unimportant in their lives, so worthy of no acknowledgment, much less, respect."

Usually I try not to hold back my own crazy or silly thinking when I react foolishly to something. Ignoring or trying to suppress such thoughts is not a good idea because the only memory that can hurt you is the one suppressed. All poignant thoughts and memories need to be remembered, because with examination, they can take the appropriate place in our psyches and lives. As a result, I let myself vent within and also have feelings of rejection and anger that even then I knew were way out of proportion to the event.

Finally, I had to laugh at myself as well as my big (yet obviously fragile) ego. This laughter also set the stage nicely for me to respond in a sensible way to the distorted thinking that the event had stirred up. As I was doing this, a version of the following old Hasidic tale that I had thought was long forgotten by me came to mind. It is amazing how the mind works at times to help us learn how to live better *if* we embrace reflections from the past that arise.

The tale began on a train. A wealthy, important businessman was riding alone in a compartment, reading a newspaper. A much older man stopped at the door to the car and motioned if he might sit down. The businessman looked up, noticed the simple clothes on the man, and thought to himself, "He looks like a beggar." And so in response, with a grimace on his face and in a stern voice, he lied by saying, "No. It is already occupied." To which the older man slightly nodded acceptance and went down the corridor to look for another seat.

At the end of the trip, as the businessman departed the train, he noticed quite a commotion several cars down. There was a very large excited crowd assembled, which made him curious as to what was happening there. He looked around for a conductor and upon finding one, asked, "What is going on down there?" "Oh, a very famous and revered rabbi was on the train and practically the whole village is out to greet him," he replied.

This intrigued the businessman even more, so he made his way down the platform and managed to weave through the crowd until he was at the front. He stood there until the rabbi walked close to him and he recognized it was the very man he rejected when approached to share his compartment. Realizing this, he quickly approached the rabbi and apologized profusely. To which the rabbi with sadness in his eyes responded in a soft voice, "Oh don't apologize to me. Find a poor man or a beggar who is dressed simply like I am and apologize to him."

Recalling this story at a time when I felt a lack of respect because of a perceived rejection of me, I was reminded of the many times I have judged people by their dress, color, language, the issues they presented, and the fears they had. I didn't look beyond the first blush of learned prejudices to see who they truly were. I didn't respect them enough to go further.

Now when I teach, supervise, or mentor professional help-ers and healers, I remember this about myself and surprise them with the comment: "Don't be sensitive to others who are different than you are." After I give them time for this to set in and see their surprised, sometimes shocked, reactions, I finally go on, "No, don't merely be sensitive to those you seek to help or heal because 'sensitivity' is often a code word for 'I'll learn their language so I can teach them my truths.' Sensitivity is not enough. We must go beyond and be willing to *learn* from everyone around us" (even those who seem not to have the time to acknowledge us during our daily walks).

Children can teach us about playfulness and mindfulness (being in the present with your eyes wide open to what is happening). Adolescents can teach us about the truth in an unvarnished way that as adults we may set aside because of our own cultural or familial norms that avoid values that might cause discomfort or prevent success. Other cultures may also be able to teach us new ways of looking at the world if only we give them a chance rather than simply label them and dismiss their teachings as "foreign" and therefore not worthy of appreciation on our part.

For us to process all of this in a natural, helpful way, however, requires that we take the time to lean back for a moment or two to learn from our emotions and ways of perceiving, thinking, and understanding. It takes time and a bit of attention to what is going on within us to learn, grow, deepen, and enjoy our lives more fully. This is especially so when we are at junctures when life is particularly stressful and challenging. Taking the time to carefully reflect and not simply ruminate can make all the difference. Otherwise, like so many around us, we can convince ourselves that rushing to our graves is the only practical way to live in today's demanding world. To make matters worse, such a style of unreflective living can result in our minds remaining contaminated with the day's heavy events, which as we shall see, can have a quite adverse impact on those with whom we interact as well.

People approach us at times with seemingly insurmountable problems. At such times, we may be tempted to pull back while thinking, "What can I do to help?" Yet it is often our simple presence to them when no answer could be sufficient or there is no "solution" to their questions. Such interactions can happen at any time.

After I finished delivering a presentation on my book *Perspective* at the 92nd Street Y in New York City, a woman approached me to ask a question in private. She said, "I am 50 years old and have just been diagnosed with what may be terminal cancer. Soon I will meet with my physicians and I am fearful of what they might say. Do you have any suggestions as to how I can deal with this fear?"

Several weeks later I was speaking to a group of health-care leaders in Indiana, once again on the topic of perspective. After my presentation, one of the executives approached me and asked if I would sign her copy of my book. I was pleased to do this because it gives me a chance to personally spend at least a little time with some of the people in the audience. As I was signing her book, she commented, "Your presentation

and this book come at just the right time for me." "How so?"
I responded. She went on to tell me that several months ago her
twenty-two-year-old son had suddenly died.

Friends, family, acquaintances, and even people we may find
ourselves sitting next to on a plane or train will sometimes
drop life's dramatic difficulties on us with a sense of question
in their voices. We erroneously think that in their doing this
they are looking for answers when in fact they are primarily
looking for someone willing to sit with them in the darkness.
Children know this almost instinctively and can teach us if,
once again, we have the willingness to learn rather than dismiss
their lessons as simplistic.

A number of years ago, I remember hearing about a woman
being quite upset because her daughter had not arrived home
on time after school. She thought she would wait a bit before
calling the school or the police. Then, just as she was ready to
contact the school, her daughter walked through the door as if
nothing had happened.

The woman's relief at seeing her turned her anxiety into
anger, so she confronted her daughter about her tardiness.
"Where were *you*? You are late. I was worried sick." To which
her daughter responded quite simply, "Oh, I was helping a
friend who was in trouble." "Well, what did you do for her?"
her mother asked. To which her daughter simply responded,
"Oh, I sat down next to her and helped her cry."

Trauma and serious stress are not primarily responded to
through employing the type of problem solving we use for daily

challenges. Significant difficulties (loss, serious illness, sexual abuse, sudden rejection) are not solvable as such, but they still can lead somewhere that provides possibly unseen benefits. This is especially so for people going through such pressures, stress, and anxiety. *If* they can encounter a clear sense of presence in another person willing to share their own inner space, eventually they can arrive at new meaning in their lives after the event.

I remember a person speaking about her mentor in such a way. She pointed out many of his gifts, but noted that in the end, it was her teacher's true ordinariness. She felt he was like a mirror for her and others to see their own gifts. Such individuals have a palpable presence that can have a major impact of its own accord—particularly if we or those we walk with are ready. As Jack Kornfield writes in his enchanting work, *After the Ecstasy, the Laundry*, "The understanding of emptiness [genuine openness, acceptance, and freedom] is contagious. It appears we can catch it from one another. We know that when a sad or angry person enters a room, we too often enter that sadness or anger. It shouldn't surprise us then, that the presence of a teacher who is empty, open, awake can have a powerful effect on another person, especially if that person is ripe."

This often translates into the ability to be "sensitive listeners" rather than simply remaining quiet until they have an opportunity to speak. Anthony Hopkins' tribute to Sir Laurence Olivier in the *New York Times* a few years ago included a number of statements, but it seemed to me to focus in particular on the great actor's sensitivity and "listening presence" to others. To illustrate this, Hopkins described his first meeting with Olivier:

> He came forward to shake my hand and I gave him my name. He gave me his full attention. This was an ability of his, to give his full, undivided attention to the moment, as if there were no past or future. Even in his "ordinariness" there was that one peculiar quality of concentration. This is what set him apart as an extraordinary human being: he never dismissed anything, he never disregarded anything. Everything held his attention.

More and more, I have begun to see how precious such a presence to others can be. This is especially so now when a chance to be heard is so rare—today everyone seems to have "answers," but few have time or the inclination to listen. When we add to this the space for people to be able to express their emotions without fear of undue reaction, rejection, or reprisals, being present to others in a nonjudgmental, accepting way can seem to be magical to the person experiencing trauma or distress.

Being a clear, reflective presence in such instances, however, is not as straightforward as it might sound. Such compassionate persons must be willing to take risks and experience both personal failure and distress themselves. Yet with the right perspective and in line with the central tenet of resiliency psychology, for those persons who do reach out with a sense of openness and intrigue, even such apparently negative encounters have the potential of producing dramatic positive results. Thus, the question anyone who is interested in fathoming the fruits of personal failure, risk, and distress must naturally ask is "What must I do to strengthen an attitude that would foster an openness to receiving new insights during dark times?" Otherwise, facing failure in inappropriate ways or simply with a sense of romanticism may only lead to greater difficulties in the future.

TWO

MINING THE FRUITS
OF PERSONAL FAILURE

*Victory, defeat—the words were meaningless. Life lies behind
these symbols and life is ever bringing new symbols into being.
One nation is weakened by a victory, another finds new forces
in defeat.*

—ANTOINE DE SAINT-EXUPÉRY, *Night Flight*

The attractiveness that modern society attributes to "success" is very alluring. But ancient and contemporary philosophers and spiritual guides have not always viewed these goals positively. For example, in 424 B.C., Aristophanes, an Athenian poet, listed three essentials for climbing the ladder of success: "to plunder, to lie . . . [and] to show your arse!"

Experiencing suffering unnecessarily when you fail is a shame. When this occurs in persons who are seeking to be compassionate with family, friends, coworkers, or as part of a professional helping role, it is truly quite sad. Unfortunately, it is all too common, especially for those in such helping professions as education, social work, ministry, mental health, the military, nursing, and medicine.

Knowing this, in working with surgical residents on ways to become and remain more resilient, I set the stage starkly for them: "Before we begin, let's face a basic fact. In your tenure as surgeons, you are going to kill people. Probably not by malpractice, but certainly by *mis*practice. You can't be on at 100% of your ability, 100% of the time. It just isn't possible no matter how good you are."

Most of us will not have to face such immense challenges as part of our work and in our personal life. However, we will have our share of darkness and will fail at times. As a matter of fact, the more we care and the greater the scope of our compassion, the more this will occur. It is a basic statistical probability: The more we are involved, the more we raise the odds that we will fail. It is as simple as that.

Consequently, our perspective on failure is essential. This is not only important for us who are in "official" caregiving and mentoring roles but also for those who count on us to remain involved—especially when the odds are great against us succeeding as we would naturally like to do. Our *attitude* is key in all of this. It will determine if we can weather the storms of failure and a sense of loss when our goals are not achieved. In her memoir, *Dakota*, author Kathleen Norris wrote that she was called to reflect on this when she had come across a handwritten note by her grandmother inserted in an old family bible. On it was written, "Keep me friendly to myself; keep me gentle in disappointment."

A Chan (Chinese Zen) master put this sense of self during failure even more pointedly when he shared, "I never regret anything I've done. I have made mistakes and will make more but in response, am clear, learn, and move on." Obviously, this is easier said than done and most of us probably wouldn't put it quite that way. In addition to being clear about what can be learned when we don't succeed, sometimes we need friends around us to help us break through and learn what benefit failure might hold for us even though no one likes to be seen in this light—especially when we feel a failure *as a person*.

A classic example of this for me is an experience reported by William Sloane Coffin, the former chaplain at Yale University. During his tenure there, he had an experience of serious marital difficulties at a time when ministers might be expected to bow out of their work if they divorced. He became so distraught that he offered his resignation to Kingman Brewster Jr., Yale's president. The temptation for Brewster to accept was there because Coffin was at times a troublesome activist. However, much to Coffin's surprise, Brewster responded by inviting him to move in with him and his wife for a while.

Coffin was still not clear as to whether he should resign or not so he took it a step further by consulting a faculty colleague, Richard Sewall. Sewall also advised him not to resign but added a compelling reason: "Bill," he said, "if you have suffered from anything, it is an aura of too much success. A little failure can only improve your ministry."

Understanding the potential value of dealing with failure is something in rare supply today. Educators who teach in schools that have a strong value system that is not only uttered but also followed can relate to this. More often than not today, parents will seek schools that they respect because of the values they hold. Yet a number of those very parents will come to the school to complain to the teachers and administrators when their children's personal and educational failures are pointed out and the student is held accountable. A student's wonderful sense of self can become distorted when both parents and the students themselves view success as the ultimate (and only) goal.

People, especially today, often live their lives in front of a mental mirror. How different such a philosophy is from that of an ancient Chinese sage who presents the following lesson on success. It is conveyed to us in Thomas Merton's *The Way of Chuang Tzu*:

> When an archer is shooting for nothing
> He has all his skill.
> If he shoots for a brass buckle
> He is already nervous.
> If he shoots for a prize of gold
> He goes blind
> Or sees two targets—
> He is out of his mind!
> His skill has not changed. But the prize
> Divides him. He cares.

> He thinks more of winning
> Than of shooting—
> And the need to win
> Drains him of power.

Failure in others' eyes can lead us to simply feel upset or it can ultimately lead to mining new leads on who we are and can be with an attitude of intrigue. As I write these words, I am reminded of an interaction I had with a quite famous and accomplished colleague many years ago.

I had received a letter from him that I thought contained information that was quite manipulative. Instead of allowing myself the time to let my emotions settle and think how I would respond, I immediately called him and let him know what I thought. In response, he said we needed to sit down and discuss this. Obviously, I had hit a nerve with him by the way I presented my feelings in a very raw way.

When we did have a chance to meet, each time I would give him an illustration as to why I was upset, he would have an answer that was less than satisfactory to me. Finally, I recognized that because I had hurt his feelings in the first place— what some in psychology would refer to as causing "narcissistic injury"—I realized I was the last person to be helping him to see how manipulative he could be at times. I also appreciated as we were discussing the events that it wasn't the lyrics (details) of what he had done that were most problematic. It was the music (style) of how he was behaving; to my mind, he was being "slick" in his approach to colleagues who had gone out of their way to work for him. Because I was obviously accomplishing nothing, I felt that the best approach would be to diffuse the emotion in the room, let go, and try to ease out of the situation.

As I was trying to do this, he looked at me and said, "You know when you called me to confront me about my actions, I called up several people and asked them about *you*." When he said this, he caught me completely off guard. At first I thought he was simply being defensive, which of course was probably partially true. However, as he said more about it, and my own defensiveness waned, the thought came to my mind that while I certainly no longer felt called to be prophetic to him about his behavior, he certainly was truly an awakening voice to me as to my own manipulative behavior and defenses.

As I stepped back from the event later that day, I also began to realize a greater point to ponder: Everything critical said to me, no matter how poor the motivation of the person sharing it might be, still contained information that would be helpful if I could approach it with a sense of intrigue rather than in a defensive or offensive way. As a result, still today, recalling that unpleasant event when I become angry, anxious, and am tempted to be angry at someone else or myself for failing a set of expectations, helps me to surface questions such as the following:

• What is *really* upsetting me about this unpleasant interaction or sense of failure?

- What am I being asked to let go of or what lesson am I being resistant to learn?
- How is my ego or insecurity preventing me from seeking what I need to observe about myself?
- What new approaches can I put into place that can prevent or lessen such a negative sense of myself or others in the future as well as prevent unnecessary mistakes?

Most people run away from looking closely at their failures—even if they are sitting by themselves at the end of the day while attempting to learn from the events, experiences, feelings, and thoughts they have. The reason is quite simple; it is unpleasant and painful at times to reflect on how we have failed. However, as French philosopher Albert Camus notes, "When a man has learned—and not on paper—how to remain alone with his sufferings, how to overcome his longing to flee, then he has little left to learn."

One of the ways people are encouraged not to run away from life's necessary darkness is to help them see the benefits of staying the course. Some of those advantages are

- increased motivation and determination to face what we experience as darkness or failure in ourselves and others;
- greater insight into our own personality style, defenses, values, gifts, and areas of vulnerability;
- less dependence on the recognition and approval of others;
- new skills and styles of behavior to complement our usual— possibly habitual—ways of interacting with others; and

- a sense of peace that is independent of external success, comfort, and security.

I must confess those thoughts didn't all come to me at once after a failure or series of them. Each time I am upset by real or perceived failure, I first need to let the "psychological dust" settle by allowing the negative emotions I felt come to the surface. This space is so important because the negative feelings will also bring along with them the dysfunctional black-and-white thinking or name-calling that are producing such unwanted, unpleasant feelings.

Failure and less satisfying interactions that open us up to our limits and denials offer information that can help us to transform our lives in a positive way. I have long felt that when I get upset at people, these very people can be the guides I need. If I can see what they are teaching me rather than simply condemning them or myself, they can call me to shape my life in a new way, facing my darkness and embracing my talents with a more complete, and thus healthier, sense of self. This can then lead to a more responsible, honest style of relating. Once again, the lesson is that anything negative said about or to us, no matter how poor the motivation of the person saying it, is true to some extent. If we are able to mine these truths, we can be freer. Moreover, this is a gift that success rarely offers us in quite the same way.

However, at some level this takes a willingness to risk seeing things and having the courage to take steps we might not

normally take. Nevertheless, one of the greatest human para-
doxes is that we seem to complain the most about a lack of passion in life and compassion for others at the very time when we
are willing to risk the least. We are challenged, for example, in
times of failure, crisis, and loss to be willing to be open to see
and act on life differently and to receive support from possibly
different sources at different times.

Given this, the overall goal of resiliency awareness is not
merely to bounce back but, in the process, also to go deeper.
To do this, however, we need to truly embrace the risks that
come with involvement. Paula McLain seems to reflect this
in her novel, *Circling the Sun*, when adventurer and pilot, Beryl
Markham, the central character says,

> I have a chart that traces my route across the Atlantic,
> Abingdon to New York, every inch of icy water I'll pass
> over, but not the emptiness involved or the loneliness, or the
> fear. Those things are as real as anything else, though, and
> I'll have to fly through them. Straight through the sicken-
> ing dips and air pockets, because you can't chart a course
> around anything you're afraid of. You can't run from any
> part of yourself, and it's better that you can't. Sometimes I've
> thought it's only our challenges that sharpen us, and change
> us, too—a mile-long runway and nineteen hundred pounds
> of fuel. Black squadrons of clouds muscling in from every
> corner of the sky and the light fading, minute by minute.
> There is no way I could do any of this and remain the same.

During the height of the sexual abuse crisis, I was asked by the Roman Catholic Archdiocese of Boston to speak to the priests about navigating psychological and spiritual darkness. The final group I was asked to address was a group of retired clergy. They were in an especially tough spot because just prior to my arrival, someone whom they respected and trusted was also accused of being an abuser. Knowing this, I tried to be both informative and gentle. As with all the persons I treat or mentor, I wanted to balance kindness with clarity. Just as I was completing the question-and-answer period and was getting ready to leave the stage, a kindly elderly priest whom I had a chance to chat with during one of the breaks raised his hand. Seeing it, I recognized him and asked, "Father, did you have a question or comment you wished to make?"

In response he said, "I would like to divinize you for the moment." I replied, "That sounds dangerous," and there was a ripple of laughter in the room. However, he went on in a very serious vein. "Given all we have been through these past few years, can you predict when this will all end?"

The room was suddenly very silent and I, myself, paused at the poignancy and import of this question. Finally after some time, I replied, "Father, even if I knew the answer to this question, I wouldn't answer it." "Why?" he asked in a puzzled voice.

"Because it is the *wrong* question." Then, after waiting a few heartbeats, I added, "The question is not, 'When will it all end?' The question is, 'What can I learn from all of this?'"

With the proper awareness, and just like failure, distress, loss, and trauma can also lead us to even more generative actions for others rather than being more involved only in ourselves to the point where we lose a healthy perspective. Examples are present in everyday people who are not psychotherapists or clinicians of some type.

In Ishinomaki, Japan, after the tsunami, a person who was relocated into a shelter shortly after his own house became uninhabitable almost immediately started sweeping out the shelter where he was crammed in with others. When asked why he did this, he replied, "No one should live like this. I just do better when I am helping other people." The point? Compassion has a place in being resilient—not simply after the fact but during it.

In the Waldo Canyon disaster in Colorado, a resident first exclaimed upon looking at the rubble that stood in place of his house, "I have lost everything!" And then after some time, he added, "No, I have lost my home of 30 years and all my *physical* possessions and this makes me sad, but I have not lost my life." The point? Developing a healthy perspective is part of resilience.

In another case, a priest who was called to a hospital to meet with parents of twins, one who was born dead, said, "When we first went to the morgue to pray over the shrouded child who had died, we cried and prayed. Then we went up to the neonatal intensive care unit and prayed beside the twin who had survived. We cried and prayed again, but this time they were prayers of joy, which I don't think I could have done had I not first cried those tears of sadness." The point? We don't gain a new perspective or deeper sense of gratitude for what is truly important in life by avoiding the sadness, trauma, or loss but by facing it directly with a sense of openness and possibility.

Examples like this then, require that we simultaneously appreciate the dangers of involvement with others while appreciating the meaning and personal return of doing it. A key problem is that because we are drawn to care for others in a professional or personal way, we set ourselves up. The seeds of personal burnout and the seeds of compassion are, in reality, the same seeds. While we don't wish to be callous, and I am not recommending that (we have enough callous people in the world already!), over-involvement with the emotions or expectations of others can prevent us from doing the very tasks we want to do for friends, family, or in the case of professionals, clients or patients. The opposite of having some emotional distance from others is not compassion but seduction. We are pulled in by the tension or upset of the moment and then are of limited use to the person we are trying to help.

There is a Russian proverb that captures the situation being described here: "When you sleep next to the cemetery, you can't cry for everyone who dies." Leaning back from the emotions experienced by others under stress, after loss, or following trauma is part of a triad: We lean back, reappraise, and then renew so we can re-enter the fray with new energy and understanding.

In Jeffrey Kottler's classic work, *On Being a Therapist*, he rightly recognizes that "The destructive energy dissipating from a patient or client pollutes the spirit of the healer. Most therapists understand they jeopardize their own emotional well-being when they intimately encounter the pain of another." He cautions those who care to appreciate that part of being compassionate includes being desensitized by human emotion and that trying to insulate ourselves from the pain of others, our own wish to perform well, or avoiding the belief that we are "special" and able to effect change that others haven't or has not been possible over a long period of time are all difficult and part of helping. I would add that these dangers apply to everyone who cares—not simply professionals.

They also imbalance our own sense of what is right and what we should be doing. I am sure I am not the only helper who has his attention wander and can't determine whether I am being too active or allowing too much time for things to take their course before reaching out. Also, there are the negative responses and efforts to destabilize our desire to reach out and help that can be painful. Two illustrations with two persons in the healing and helping professions quickly come to mind: one with a Catholic nun and the other with a psychotherapist.

The nun was sent to me by her religious congregation for a psychotherapeutic evaluation. It seems there was great anger toward her by her other community members. The cause was her own negative style of interacting according to her local religious superior. When I went out into the waiting room to meet her for a first visit and to introduce myself, she saw me, looked up, and frowned. I smiled and said, "Sister, we haven't even begun the treatment and you're giving me dirty looks." To which she responded, "That is why they sent me here." To which I smiled again and said, "Well, let's go into my office and chat because I can't charge you for what we are doing out here," finally eliciting laughter and a smile on her part. Once she was able to share her story, describe her angry interactions, and we were able to explore what she had experienced over the past several years in terms of dramatic, unwanted, and frightening change that had never been understood by her or others, I could see what was really going on. She was not suffering from an angry heart; she was suffering from a broken heart. Unfortunately, neither she nor the persons she lived with clearly understood this.

A similar case occurred with a psychotherapist who was poorly treated in her work environment. I was asked to mentor her through what she was experiencing and I must confess, because of her anger and sarcasm, it wasn't easy. The emotional scene with her could change so quickly. On one occasion, she came into the room and said to me that she had read my book *Riding the Dragon* and really loved it. I was surprised by this positive comment and thanked her. To which she quickly added, "Too bad you're not like what you've written." Within me, two reactions quickly followed one another. The first was a natural negative reaction to hearing something like that. The second was to see how such responses in the past pushed people away or had them respond in kind. Knowing that in therapy and mentoring, the goal is not to react but to reflect within and then between the two of you, I said, "From your words and the tone in your voice, it sounds like you feel I've let you down in some way. Maybe we can speak about that."

Anyone who reaches out to others, be they professionals or someone simply trying to be a good parent or is caring for a spouse, sibling or one's own parent, or simply acting upon the desire to help coworkers and those in need who cross their paths, must recognize that having a caring attitude can be dangerous to one's own sense of commitment to what we know is good. For instance, a number of years ago, a large search was undertaken for a chancellor for a major university system. After a long and arduous process, he was chosen, only to have him resign after less than a year in office. When asked about this, he said that it wasn't anything major that was overwhelming. It was the "gnats" that got to him. The constant bickering, complaints, obstructions, minor hostilities, hypersensitivity, and such stresses sapped his energy and made him feel overwhelmed, underappreciated, and drained of creativity.

One of my own senior colleagues seemed to recognize and know how to handle this reality even though the patients he saw in his clinical practice were some of the most psychologically difficult you could treat. I once asked him what his secret was in not simply surviving but actually thriving as a psychologist. He looked at me, smiled, and said, "Bob, there are really only five annoying, extremely needy patients in the whole country."

When I gave him a quizzical look, he then added, "They just travel from clinical practice to clinical practice and they are coming to yours *next!*" and he laughed.

His humor was one of the saving graces that helped him keep a healthy perspective. However, it was more than that, and I could sense it in what he quickly added, this time with a serious expression on his face: "Bob, when we see patients or clients that are very demanding, quickly turn on us even when we have gone the extra mile and then some to help them, we must always remember that this is the best they can do and not take it personally." He then added, "You are a very talented person, therapist, and mentor, but all of us fail at times no matter how talented we may be. I still remember what President Jimmy Carter's mom who volunteered in India once said when she was discouraged about the way one of her adult children was behaving, "There are times when I look around at my children and think, 'I should have remained a virgin!'" My colleague's humor was precious and filled with enough insight for me to see he wasn't just making fun of things or me but helping me realize how tough it is to care for others and how important it is to do what we can, including using humor, to maintain a healthy perspective. But even more than this, he was reminding me not to personalize the negative responses from persons who were going through so much. With what they were experiencing, they were doing the best they could. The goal in being compassionate to others is to have *low expectations and high hopes.*

People who are born helpers need to realize that they will never get used to failure, not simply because they wish to be successful, as enjoyable as that is, but because they hate to see people suffer—especially when it is unnecessary. The most that can be expected is that they will be able to develop the "psychological scar tissue" that comes from being in tough situations, sitting alongside those who are crying, angry, depressed, under great stress, and grieving over a great loss. Yet even then, the occupational hazard of being compassionate will catch up with us at times. When we care for others, as professionals or as part of our everyday lives, we must recognize that "compassionate impairment" or "secondary stress" (the pressures we experience in reaching out to others) is usually a quiet slow process rather than the result of a cataclysmic event.

I remember coming home one day after a full day of clinical practice. When I walked in the door, my wife asked me, "How was your day?" In response I said, "Terrible." She was surprised and asked, "Well, what happened today?" After sitting down and thinking about it, I replied, "Nothing awful." And, when she asked, "Well, why did you respond that way?" I said, "Because when you asked that question, my response was that I wanted to cry." After thinking about it for a while, I realized what was going on. It was nothing dramatic in the moment. Instead, over the day, week, month, and maybe the year, I had absorbed people's sadness, futility, feelings they were not understood, depression, stress, and anxiety. What I needed at that moment was contemplative Thomas Merton's recommendation, "Courage comes and goes. Hold on for the next supply."

If we are willing to ride the waves of compassion, then we will be thrown off our normal game at times. This is to be expected even if we are careful, alert, and seek to have the right balance in our lives. It is how we bounce back at these crucial points that makes the difference.

I think the following words of American ethicist, theologian, and commentator Reinhold Niebuhr help us put our efforts in perspective when we face failure, take risks, and address trauma experienced by others. He said, "Nothing we do, however virtuous, can be accomplished alone . . ." Knowing this will come about when we take time to realize that faithfulness doesn't necessarily bring with it success and that failure actually teaches us so much if we face it in the correct manner. Yet facing it is not a once-and-for-all action. It is also not something that will be possible without leaning back psychologically so we can create refreshing emotional space within to gain a sense of a world that is freer and more spacious, no matter what is going on around us.

THREE

―――――

FROM A HEALTHY DISTANCE

*My feelings deepened and lingered. The swift moods of early
childhood—each formed by and suited to its occasion—vanished.
Now feelings lasted so long they left stains. They arose from
nowhere, like winds or waves, and battered me or engulfed me.*
—ANNIE DILLARD, *An American Childhood*

*For most of us, our chief orientation in life is this more or less
continuous stream of mental and physical activity. When that
becomes disrupted, we may get brief glimpses of a freer, more
spacious world.*
—CLARK STRAND, *The Wooden Bowl*

There is a piece of classical Eastern wisdom that gently
encourages us to see that, if we can lean back, take a
breath, relax, and be comfortable with ourselves, we can travel
anywhere. Nowhere is such guidance of greater essence than
when we walk with others through their own personal darkness
and we feel the negative impact of it as well.

A number of years ago, I was asked to deliver a presentation
on resiliency to U.S. Army chaplains and chaplain assistants in

Germany whom I knew were under great stress. Many of them had just returned from the war zones in Afghanistan and Iraq. Just as I was to walk up on the stage to begin, a colonel walked up to me and said, "Before you begin, I just wanted to share with you a caution." "What is it?" I asked. He said, "There are a lot of ghosts in this room. There is nothing left inside them."

His statement brought me back to a passage in the novel, *The Case of Lucy Bending*. In it, Lawrence Sanders writes, "Most laymen, he supposed believed psychiatrists fell apart under the weight of other people's problems. Dr. Theodore Levin had another theory. He feared that a psychiatrist's life force gradually leaked out. It was expended on sympathy, understanding, the obsessive need to heal and help create whole lives. Other people's lives. But always from the outside. Always the observer. Then one day he would wake up and discover that he himself was empty, drained."

I think this is the case not simply with professional helpers and healers but with any truly compassionate person. The difference with the professionals, however, is that they are trained to take some space during the day and week to debrief themselves. Although some let this process slip and, of course, eventually pay the psychological price for it. Even though my work with caregivers in dramatically dark situations has made me alert to what is going on within me as well as between me and my patients and those I supervise, failing to be attuned to the psychological dangers of helping befalls us all at times.

When the tragedies of September 11 happened, I was living outside of Washington, D.C. Because of my work, I was often dealing with other people's pain and not taking much note of my own. Finally, I realized that I needed to do two things. First, in the long run, I needed to strengthen my "self-care protocol," the program of renewing elements that would not only replenish my energy but allow me to keep the challenges facing me in perspective. (See *Bounce* or *The Resilient Clinician* for a more detailed description of a self-care protocol.) Second, I knew myself well enough to know that it was also important for me to do something more immediate to short-circuit my stress and give me the space to reflect, renew, and feel more resilient.

Because I know that one of the sources of distress is the feeling that we are being controlled by habit and are prisoners of our intense schedules, I looked at what could be postponed, shortened, or avoided the next day. From experience, I knew that by finding and expanding moments of mindfulness (being reflectively present in the moment), it would have immediate beneficial results. At least it had done so for me until now.

With this plan in mind, I was able to cancel some meetings, postpone a few, and shorten others. I also decided to avoid rising at 5:00 a.m. for quiet centering time and instead "sleep in" until 8:00. However, life had other plans for me that day and in the following days as well, because the planned day of renewal began not at 8:00 with a leisurely cup of coffee but at 5:30 a.m. with a phone call to tell me that a tornado had struck Maryland.

Half in a fog from having been abruptly awakened, I replied, "That's terrible, but why are you calling me?" The caller responded, "Because the mother of the two university students killed in the storm are daughters of someone who teaches with your wife." And that was the way my "semi day of renewal" started.

Following this, I went into the office and I opened up the email list to find one from someone at the Pentagon discussing stress being experienced after the plane had struck it. I responded to him, turned around, and a colleague entered who had just returned from undertaking debriefing of staff members at the White House who were under a great deal of stress. After debriefing her about what she experienced, the phone rang as she was walking out the door, and it turned out to be my wife who explained that her older sister in New York City, who was at the heart of the family, had just died.

This time, surprisingly to me as I look back at it now from a distance, I didn't realize—possibly because I was so focused on others—that all of this was taking a toll on me. It finally hit me when I traveled to New York for my sister-in-law's funeral. Shortly after I arrived at the funeral parlor, one of my nephews, who knows what I do and is a fireman there, said, "Uncle Bob, I am sure you want to hear about what went on at Ground Zero." As he related what went on in the immediate aftermath of the planes hitting the Twin Towers, I still wasn't fully aware of the combined impact of all I had encountered in the past several days until he said, "And then there were the dogs, Uncle

Bob." "What about the dogs, Larry?" "They are trained to find people alive," he said. Then he added, "But everyone was *dead*. They became so depressed that they wouldn't drink water on site, so we had to evacuate them to feed them fluids intravenously so they wouldn't die."

Hearing this, I finally realized the toll all of this was taking on me. In response, I did what I normally do when I feel myself emotionally being totally overwhelmed, I asked the detail question, "Where did you evacuate them to?" In retrospect, I know that I really didn't care where they evacuated the dogs to but needed to ask an intellectual question to stop the emotional slide. I finally could see clearly that I needed some distance from the stories, emotions, helplessness, trauma, and stress at hand.

In place of these events in my life at that point, anyone of us could fill in the blanks with other, equally disabling distress-points. Maybe it is a parent or spouse who is demonstrating early signs of Alzheimer's disease, an adolescent child who is on drugs, serious financial problems, the ramifications of a divorce, being sued for malpractice, personal physical problems, or a new supervisor or position, which are unexpectedly toxic or unreasonably demanding. All of this takes a toll that must be appreciated and faced.

Most of us don't realize how emotionally contaminated we can become as a result of certain interactions during the day. Sometimes it is caused by contact with other's experience of loss, pain, or injustice or seemingly being rebuffed that infects

us. In the case of those who are professional healers and helpers, it can be a series of more dramatic encounters that may
take their toll on them and even their families and friends if
left unchecked. Just as professional caregivers must learn to
deal with what faces them, everyone in today's challenging
world would do well to follow in their footsteps by taking a
few moments to let the dust of the day settle. Surprisingly, even
those who are in intense helping roles sometimes forget or don't
think to do this.

At the height of both the Iraqi and Afghani wars, a surgeon from Walter Reed Army Hospital shared with me what
seemed to be an unsolvable dilemma for him. He told me, "I
am under great stress. Because of it, my family is suffering as
well. Everything is a mess. I have come off a recent deploy-
ment. I am sure I have another one facing me down the road
and all I seem to do now is cut people's legs off. I would just
like to take a gall bladder out for a change. Then when I go
home, I try to calm down by hitting a few golf balls into a
cup upstairs in my home office, and my wife barges into the
room and accuses me of ignoring her and the children when
I do it. I am not sure my marriage is going to last if all of this
keeps up."

I asked him, "Well what do you do when work is done?"

He gave me a surprised look and said, "Why go right home,
of course."

"Well you can't do that if you want to make it in military
medicine."

"What do you mean? What *should* I do?" You could tell from the tone in his voice he also was now frustrated and angry with me.

I replied, "Well when you go into a restaurant bathroom there is always a sign that says, 'Restaurant personnel must wash their hands before going back to work.' You know better than I do that when we work in the hospital, we must not only wash our hands after we go to the bathroom but also *before*, so we don't contaminate ourselves with what we might have physically been in touch with on the floors. The same can be said about us psychologically. And so when you are done with work before you go home you need to emotionally decontaminate yourself."

"How do I accomplish that?"

"Nothing too involved or fancy. Just walk around the hospital when you are done working. If people are only going to stop you when you do this to ask you a question or make a comment, then walk outside on the hospital grounds or drive to a place where you can stretch your legs or simply sit in the car alone for a while."

"Then, when you get home, apologize to your wife. Tell her, 'You are right. I have not paid full attention to you and the children for a while because of what has been happening at work. You deserve better and so do I. I am missing out on really being with all of you instead of always being preoccupied with work as if you, the children, and enjoying our family life isn't as important. So here is what I am going to do.

I am going to take a few moments to take a walk after I leave work to calm down. Then, when I come home I will first go upstairs and take off my uniform so I can leave that role back at work. After that, I will putt a few golf balls upstairs by myself for a few moments, not because I want to ignore you and the children, but so I can really come down from all that is going on at the hospital so we can truly be together as a family again."

All of us, not simply those in the intense helping professions, need this type of space at the end of the day so we can decompress; shed ourselves of the feelings, thoughts, and events of the day; and clean our psychological palate. Simply by taking out a little time to mentally move away from the workaday world and get some space, we can decontaminate ourselves from the negativity and pressures experienced. This will not only allow us to avoid carrying what has been a burden at work into our homes but will also prevent us from inflicting these experiences on those we love or encounter in our personal lives. Further, it will help us appreciate our limits, shift mental gears to what renews or challenges us in different ways after work, and help us take ourselves a little less seriously in settings where this makes a great deal of sense. Otherwise our roles may get confused, and we will run the risk of becoming CEOs to our families and parents or spouses to those with whom we work, which sets us up for potential interpersonal disaster. Instead, we need refreshing emotional space within ourselves so we don't fall prey to such behavior.

A key to a life of meaning and compassion—especially when faced with our own and others' intense emotions—is to take some space to let what we are feeling settle before we respond. Whereas many people tend to react immediately or deny what they are feeling in volatile settings, those who are taught to care for others are psychologically taught to lean back and reflect, first within themselves and then between themselves and the other persons present. However, it is easy to forget this lesson, no matter what your training.

An American Buddhist nun pulled me aside after a presentation I was giving in Cambodia on self-care. She was concerned about a young Buddhist protégé who was working in a hospital there, which cared for villagers who had lost limbs when they stepped on land mines in what they thought were cleared areas. The mines were made of plastic and during floods would travel back into areas previously swept clean, catching them unawares. The Friends Committee responded to this horrible situation by providing prosthetic devices to those in the hospital so they could walk and work again. Obviously, this was important not only from a financial point of view to the amputees but a psychological one as well. The nun said the toll on the young man was tremendous.

When I asked her what happened when as a Buddhist he meditated after his day's work before he got in the car to return home, she gave me a sad, stunned look. She then said, "You would think that as a Buddhist I would have immediately recognized the value of meditation and suggested it to him.

However, I made the mistake of seeing this practice as something we only do during designated times. I forgot the value
of it in *all* situations—especially tough ones where we need to
allow the dark dust of the day to settle."

When we take time in silence and solitude, possibly in
meditation, we are able to gain distance from what we are
facing at the time. There is an emptying (*kenosis*) of ourselves,
we see better how our egos are demanding so much attention
and preventing us from seeing, hearing, and experiencing life
more fully and clearly. Rather than being in a cognitive cocoon
where we are disputing the past and mentally arguing with a
cast of characters in our heads, we let the dust settle and feel
the refreshing breath that is only possible in the now. This is
not only important for our own well-being but so that we will
be fresh enough to be available to others.

My own daughter was in the hospital for surgery when she
was young. It would involve having thirteen levels of her spine
fused and a rod inserted as the treatment protocol for severe
scoliosis. I did not take time to "psychologically lean back" so
I could process my own anxiety but instead came directly to
the hospital carrying the worry on my face. When my daughter
saw my expression, she looked up and said, "Dad, you look
worse than I feel!" At that moment, I realized not only had
I not taken time out for myself but that I was in no position to
support my daughter who was the person who most needed it.

When I deal with persons in the helping and healing professionals, as well as interact with caring family members or

coworkers, I don't worry whether they care enough. I am usually concerned that they care too much. By that I mean that they have not taken care of themselves and distanced themselves from the emotions they must face. In doing this, they set themselves up to be overwhelmed and to become helpless. Certainly, everyone who needs surgery would want their surgeons to care about their welfare, but they wouldn't want them to care so much that their ability to help is compromised. None of us wants to see our surgeon crying as we are being wheeled into the operating room!

When helpers and healers are in training, they are taught the importance of gaining a distance from those they are helping. This is not so they become callous. Instead they are taught that the opposite of detachment is not compassion but vulnerability to being pulled in by the emotion and often unrealistic expectations of those they are trying to help. Detachment is actually part of a triad: We sense becoming emotional and psychologically lean back; we reappraise why we are feeling this way and how to tone our emotions down; and finally, we put into action steps to renew so we can re-enter the situation feeling clearer and stronger about what we can do and what we can't.

A patient once said to me, "I notice that you laugh with me but you don't cry. However, I finally realized that you must cry at times, but you don't do it in front of me." She was very perceptive. There are times when I do feel overwhelmed. However, I have worked hard on not losing control in the room and, in the process, burdening the patient with my own feelings.

One patient of mine who had been in Beirut during a bombing said that he went into individual therapy but finally had to leave and find a new therapist. When I asked him why, he said that when he shared his stories of the carnage and upset, his therapist would get upset. It was only when he found a clinician who could remain distant enough from his pain that treatment began to be successful.

The same is worth being remembered by anyone seeking to reach out to others in need. Without the ability to have space within and a distance from the pain of even those close to us, it is hard to be clear, helpful, and know the limits of what can be done—even though we may wish to do more for our children, siblings, parents, other family members, friends, coworkers, or acquaintances.

A key aspect of being able to do this is to take the space to reflect and decompress. Even people who are overwhelmed initially can do constructive things when they have taken the time to let the "psychological dust" settle. For instance, after the terrible devastation caused by a tsunami in Ishinomaki, Japan, a woman was able to contribute not only to her own sense of control but also help others find beauty and perspective through her efforts. Within the rubble outside her house, she realized it was not quantity but symbolic quality that was needed. And so she planted flowers outside her house so she could look out and see life and beauty not just destruction. This also supported her neighbors' efforts to find a light in the darkness as well.

In a situation closer to home, my daughter who had the severe operation for scoliosis when she was young, had the rod taken out because of excruciating pain when she was in university. Several years later she almost died giving birth to her second child. By taking time out after each event to lean back and process it, she was able to let her own suffering soften her rather than make her become bitter. This became evident later in life when she told me something I didn't know: "Dad, I always wanted to be a Marine Corps officer like you were." She saw the surprise on my face and continued by adding, "However, as you know, this was impossible since I had so many physical problems." When I asked how she dealt with her disappointment, she responded, "I decided to become a social worker and seek a position in the Veterans Administration." She could see by the expression on my face how proud I was of her. This feeling of gratitude for the woman my little girl had become was to be magnified later when she did, in fact, gain a position with the Department of Veterans Affairs (VA).

After several years with the VA she was assigned to work with severely injured veterans returning from Iraq and Afghanistan. In that role she was approached by a young man who had just returned. She smiled at him and welcomed him with the empathy that I think only someone who has endured great suffering and taken the time to transform it into something useful can by saying, "You have served our country well. Now, you come on in and let us know what we can do for you."

Pacing ourselves in how we deal with what is painful around us is not running away. It is respecting that the self is limited and can only deal with so much. Such respect involves understanding what Dorothee Sölle from Germany once said, "There are two kinds of pain. One is avoidable. That you must avoid. The other is unavoidable. That you must face."

A military physician once said to me that one thing I told him when I spoke at Walter Reed army hospital made all the difference in his keeping emotionally afloat. I was curious as to what it was, thinking it was a dramatic insight I had possibly offered based on my experience, so I asked him which comment had been particularly helpful. In response he said, "I mentioned that after I returned from Iraq, I was very upset by the constant coverage of the war that I saw on TV. After I told you that and asked what I should do, you said, 'Well, when you see war coverage coming on, shut the damn thing off!'" We need to have an asceticism of burdens so we don't feel we need to carry everyone's pain or have the dysfunctional belief that people will appreciate our presence to them or actually follow our guidance. It is simply giving with a sense of *mitzvah*—giving what we can when we can and expecting nothing in return— that is the key to remaining compassionate with others on an ongoing basis.

I worked in Beirut with caregivers who were living and working in Aleppo, Syria during the height of the bombings in 2015. Some of those who had come to me for help expressed their feelings that I could not be of use to them because I was not living under the same conditions as they were. It made no difference to them that I had worked in Cambodia with members of nongovernmental organizations (NGOs) and was also a therapist to relief workers who had been evacuated from the bloody genocide in Rwanda. This was because the Syrian workers were experiencing "traumatic transference." This term, used by some therapists, refers to a feeling of helplessness that occurs when helpers are dealing with extremely dire situations. The Syrian caregivers had to contend daily with persons experiencing terror and destruction, who were unable to adequately protect themselves and had no one to hear their cries for help during the traumatic events. They now turned to the helpers who had come to me for help. In the case of some of these caregivers, their response was to feel they must be omnipotent caregivers because of the fantasy of those who came to see them that they could make everything better. As a result, these helpers often fell prey to taking on more of an advocacy role than was reasonable or began to fall victim to aspirations to be able to take care of everything, understand everything, and be able to feel a sense of love for everyone who came through the door for help.

Because such actions and attitudes are not possible—even if you are a helper—the result was a sense of impotence and anger. Now that they felt safely in the presence of their colleagues and me, they expressed their anger and powerlessness by indicating that it was impossible for me to understand and therefore help them. This was a natural expression of "traumatic countertransference" where helpers mimic their own clients or patients to the person seeking to support them.

Because I had spent time in silence and solitude, wrapped in gratitude for all that was good in my life, and did not have the expectations that I could satisfy their needs or expectations but could do something to help if I didn't become overwhelmed in the process, I was able to lean back psychologically when confronted with their feelings. I knew they were experiencing "parallel process," in which helpers themselves experience acute secondary stress because of the problems they are dealing with and then unconsciously seek to do the same thing to those supervising them—in this case, *me.*

Knowing this, and having taken time to have space within myself, allowed me to open up a space for them to vent their feelings of helplessness and anger at their terrible situations. Then, once this space was allowed and used by them, I could then let them know that (as in the case of a male obstetrician who can't possibly feel the pain of his patients yet still help) I could offer help that they certainly deserved.

The journey in seriously entering into a practice of mindfulness meditation began for me more than thirty years ago during a tough period in my own life. As I was seeking to help people deal with personal burnout, I was feeling a sense of emotional depletion in my own life. In response, I decided to seek mentoring from psychologist and spiritual writer, Henri Nouwen, flew to Boston where Nouwen was teaching at the time, and visited him in his little apartment off Harvard Square.

Among the topics that came up was the importance of being centered as I entered the day, especially because my work with persons in the helping and healing professions here in the United States and abroad could be so intense. A simple, but profound, suggestion he made was that I should try taking about twenty minutes each morning for what is widely referred to now as "mindfulness meditation." This simple practice of being in silence and solitude immediately after I arose, with no agenda other than to relax, breathe deeply, while sitting up straight, was both renewing and enlightening.

The experience was often a little like the one performing artist and composer David Bowie said he had when he entered the Strand Bookstore in London: "It's impossible to find the book you want, but you always find the book you didn't know you wanted." Like the Strand, I would often enter meditation with all kinds of thoughts and desires, fears and resentments, questions and confusion. I would let all of these thoughts and feelings move through me like a train. I tried not to entertain or suppress them but simply notice their passing. When the mental dust settled, as it usually eventually did, the busy mind would finally relax. Just as with turbulent water once the winds of concern, ego-centeredness, and a desire to control settled, clarity came about. The silence and solitude were renewing at that point, in and of itself. Yet entering these periods with no expectations allowed the silence to speak and teach me the unexpected. This was clearly something not possible during most of the day when I was trapped in an envelope of my own thoughts and judgments.

Time spent in silence and solitude on a regular basis can also affect us by

- sharpening our sense of clarity about the life we are living and the choices we are making;
- enhancing our attitude of simplicity as we have the space to pare things down and uncover central themes
- increasing our humility, which helps us avoid unnecessary arrogance by allowing time to examine the defenses and games we play as these will surface given enough quiet time;
- letting us enjoy our relationship with ourselves more as well as decreasing our dependence on the reinforcement of others;
- enabling us to recognize our own gifts and talents as well as our own areas of anger, entitlement, greed, and cowardice once we give ourselves the opportunity to quietly review the day's activities and our reactions to them;
- protecting our own inner fire so we can continue to reach out to others without being pulled down;
- helping us to have the time and space alone to accept change and loss;
- making us more sensitive to our compulsions and habits; and
- allowing us to surface attitudes of blaming others and condemning ourselves so such outlooks can be pruned, and

we can become more intrigued about how and why we do something so that ineffective styles can be altered.

In essence then, what has come to mind during moments of spaciousness, I believe has helped me to be clearer; to see my foibles with a sense of gentle humor or intrigue; to let me renew and accept change, grieve losses, enjoy my own company more, and *unlearn* what may have been helpful in the past but is no longer useful. This last process ("unlearning"), however, takes a bit more attention outside of meditation. The meditation must somehow positively contaminate the rest of my day with a new appreciation of how openness to seeing differently can make even what is routine both fresh and refreshing. Unlearning is worthy of study in and of itself.

FOUR

REMOVING THE PSYCHOLOGICAL CATARACTS

When you are fooled by something else,
the damage will not be so big.
But when you are fooled by yourself,
it is fatal. No more medicine.

—SHUNRYU SUZUKI

O ne of my favorite cartoons is from the *New Yorker* magazine. It depicts parents saying goodbye to their son as he walks, with a suitcase in one hand and a guitar in the other, under the entryway arch onto the university's grounds for the first time. Both parents are seen waving goodbye, with the father yelling to him, "Be afraid to try new things!"

Most of us would smile at this. Practically all of us, if asked whether we would be willing to try new things, would respond in the affirmative. Yet habit and ingrained beliefs about what is good or bad most often prevent us from even noticing possibilities that might be present.

One of the joys of traveling abroad to offer presentations and workshops is that I often have an opportunity during a break in the program to see some of the country through the eyes of the people who live there. In a trip to Guatemala City to work with those helping the tortured and abused indigenous poor of the country, I was asked if I would like to visit the garden spot of Antigua not far from the city.

I was glad for the break and the opportunity. After driving to and touring the town for a couple of hours, I was asked if I would like to stop for lunch. I said I would love to and threw in the off-handed question, "How far is the restaurant you have chosen?" To my surprise, my guide responded, "Right here," gesturing to a high stone wall. I gave him a puzzled look and said, "Where?" He laughed, went a few feet further, and reached over and opened a small door in the wall. I followed him through it and was surprised to find an open-air restaurant with tables set among gardens and a woman in the corner intently making fresh tortillas on a grill, all of which made me smile broadly. Then to complete the scene, just as we sat down, a mariachi band that I hadn't seen in another part of the garden started playing the rich, uplifting music for which they are known. If I hadn't been with someone who knew the area, I certainly would have missed the little door and sign by it announcing a restaurant within that would deserve at least a peek if I had been attentive enough to notice it.

Attentiveness is often missing because people confuse it with the activity of concentration that involves a focusing on something or someone. Attention is the act of being present and mindful so we don't see as much through our own lenses of judgment or our desires, needs, or value systems. It is a relaxed alertness that allows us to simply lean back and observe what is.

Agatha Christie's fictional detective, Miss Marple, refers to herself in one of the episodes as "a noticing sort of person." That is what those in the helping and healing professions do when they are in good form. A therapist can see that although a person is saying he is happy about his new promotion, the troubled expression on his face and the anxious tone of his voice are saying something else. When a student explains to a teacher the route she took to solving a mathematical problem, the teacher can tell whether or not the student understands the concept by observing the student's body language. And through observing the different reported symptoms and physical signs, a physician can determine the particular syndrome the patient is suffering from. Attention is necessary when we reach out to others or reach within ourselves in an effort to observe what is going on with respect to our own reactions, feelings, cognitions, and beliefs. Whether we are professionals or not, if we wish to reach out to others, we need to be like Miss Marple, a "noticing sort of person."

However, if we are to work in difficult situations, we must also be willing to go beyond this. We must be willing to have a radical sense of openness that goes beyond simply seeing what we can see at the moment. We must be willing to *un*learn, so possibilities can arise that we might have missed if we weren't willing to entertain what is truly new and not previously experienced. In the "psychological darkness" and trauma of situations, we must also be alert to where we can experience the "light of hope"—not in romantic ways, but in surprising ways that reflect the theme of true hope.

As Václav Havel, the former poet-leader of the Czech Republic, once recognized: "Hope is an orientation of the spirit, an orientation of the heart. It is not the conviction that something will turn out well, but the certainty that something makes sense, regardless of how it turns out." More than this though, with the correct "eyes" or perspective, we can recognize new strength in those we serve as well as grow as persons ourselves.

When I visited Cambodia for the first time to offer presentations on resilience, they were having an especially difficult time. Months earlier the Vietnamese had invaded and pushed the ruthless Khmer Rouge regime north. Now the United Nations had sent in a force to stabilize the country prior to their upcoming elections. The temporary government installed by the Vietnamese was running a slate, as was a party supporting the king who had returned, and even the Khmer Rouge, if you can believe it, were offering candidates.

I was instructed to fly to Bangkok where I would meet a contact from a relief organization who would then give me my plane tickets. The person giving them to me was a seasoned China hand who at one point had been put under house arrest in Shanghai by Mao Zedong during the long march south. When she gave me my tickets, I was surprised because they were on SK Air, which was an airline I had never heard of.

I told her that I would feel more secure on Thai Air since I had flown them before and they were great. She then said something I would hear again and again when I was overseas at the request of a relief agency: "We got a good deal on the tickets!" When I questioned her further about this, she said, "I have flown it and you will love it!" By the look on her face, I knew she meant it. However, since at one time she had been under house arrest in China and faced many trials, I knew this would be a true lesson in perspective for me given my primarily first-world experiences with airways.

When I went to the airport the next morning, my fears were confirmed. The plane was an old plane that was freshly painted. As I looked at it with concern, a fellow from the United Nations, identifiable by his blue beret, standing next to me could see my expression and laughed. I asked, "What is it?" He replied, "It is an old Russian Tupolev jet; you're in for a ride!"

He was right. As I boarded the plane, I could see that the tires were worn down to the canvas. When I sat down in my seat and looked up, I could see that the flap above me was bolted shut. No mask was going to drop if the air pressure changed. When I turned around to look for the nearest exit as they advise you to do on flights in the States, I saw that next to the exit door was a box, again freshly painted, this time with the words, "Escape rope." Finally, when we landed in Phnom Penh, all the empty seats went forward as on an old bus. Yes, given all of this and the fact it didn't bother the old China hand when she flew it reminded me that life is certainly a matter of perspective.

Once landed, I was met by someone from the hosting organization. As I got into the van, he said to me, "Is there anything you would like before I take you to the hotel?" I said, "Yes, I would like a briefing on the stress."

"Didn't you get one over the phone?"

"I did, but I want to experience the stress I am going to speak about."

"How much do you want to experience?"

"Give me the full dose?"

He smiled a bit and said, "Well, given what is going on, we can go out on the Mekong and be shot at."

I smiled back at him and said, "Let's aim a little lower than that."

He then just nodded and indicated he would take me to two places that would give me a sense of what life was like there. The first of these was what is known as "the Killing Fields." When I arrived I was surprised for a number of reasons. First, there were few people at the site even though it was a memorial to such a horrendous time in the history of both the country and the world. Second, I was shocked to see the main monument. It was a large, glass, rectangular tower that contained one type of specimen: people's skulls. I must confess I found it hard to take in, so I simply stood quietly and reverently in front of it for a few moments.

Then I looked around the site and saw excavations in the distance. Deciding I wanted to see what was in those holes, I walked over to them. As I was walking, I could hear a crunching noise, so I bent down and scraped the ground to find the source of the sound. It was then that I realized that I was walking over the bits of bones of some of the 1½ million people of the 6 million people of Cambodia who were tortured and killed during the Khmer Rouge rule.

The following trip was to Tuol Sleng, which was a high school that had been used as a torture chamber by the Khmer Rouge. When we got to the setting, the driver said to me, "Doc, I am not going to go in with you." I said, "Oh, you don't want to go in?" "No," he replied. "You see it was my high school and both my parents were tortured and killed here in Tuol Sleng." I nodded briefly and after looking at him quietly for a few seconds said, "Well, I'll be out shortly."

When I entered the schoolyard, I looked up and could see that they had meshed in the second floor veranda with barbed wire so persons imprisoned could not commit suicide while they were being tortured. I then entered the building and had to wait until my eyes adjusted because they had divided the schoolrooms into cells with the dark wood from the area. When I could see more clearly, I noticed the blood stains still on the floors and walls. Finally, when I walked back into the schoolyard, I stood there in the bright sun, sweating from the high humidity and thought to myself, "How are these people going to survive this? How are they going to survive this? The whole country must be experiencing PTSD [posttraumatic stress disorder]."

My initial sense was that the main challenge for me would be to be able to steadfastly keep a healthy sense of perspective while surrounded with such darkness. Fortunately, I was able to maintain a sense of openness to the possibility for more than this, because as it turned out, the main lesson was to be something else.

Later that day, I went with a Catholic priest on his journey across the Mekong to visit a community of Vietnamese who had lived and worked in Buddhist Cambodia for many years. Some had been born there or came to Cambodia so young that they didn't even remember their early years in Vietnam. As we approached the river, the priest said to me, "I don't know if you want to go across with me. I just noticed some government troops looking through the fields. It seems that some of the Khmer Rouge are making incursions into the south and the troops have told me they are burning out Vietnamese villagers so they won't vote in the upcoming elections." I remembered from my days as a Marine Corps officer that when it is dangerous on one side of the river, it probably is dangerous on the other side as well. So rather than stay here alone and supposedly safe, I might as well get a free boat ride out of it!

After crossing the Mekong, we met a man who shared with us that he had been burned out. He said through dual interpreters—Vietnamese to Khmer to English—that his house had been torched and he had lost everything. He had only the clothes on his back left. While he was telling this story, I looked around the village and saw that instead of 570 families there to greet the priest who was to celebrate a liturgy for them, there were only about 70 left. The rest had broken down their houses, put them in long boats, and went back to Vietnam for safety—a home that few of them really knew.

As we walked through the village to the church, a young girl who walked alongside me obviously wanted my attention. As I stretched out my hand and she grasped it, her whole face seemed to smile and her eyes widened with delight. After the priest celebrated Mass for them, we had a light lunch and then walked back and got into the boat. The little girl got in for a ride with us as did the older man whose house had been burned down. (We found out later that he was the little girl's father.)

As we pushed off and I looked into their eyes, I realized I was struck by their resilience. In the little girl's eyes, instead of seeing the dull look of PTSD that I sometimes see in children, there was a spark of hope even after all she had been through as a young child. The man's demeanor also struck me because he had that look of defiance that seemed to say: "You can burn my house, take my belongings, and maybe at some point, my life, but you will never take my spirit! Not on this watch you won't!"

The experiences I had with this older man and young girl reminded me of the words of Dorothee Sölle: "There are two kinds of suffering. The first kind is avoidable. Avoid it. The second kind is unavoidable and that you must face."

All of this would come to me again when I heard about a physician from Doctors Without Borders, who worked in Somalia during the height of the starvation. He was asked by an interviewer from National Public Radio in the United States, how he could stand such horrors—the older people were dropping like flies from lack of food, and the children were dying at such a fast rate that they were initially stacking them up in the corner like firewood. To this he first responded with a question: "When you see this carnage on television in the U.K., America, Australia, New Zealand, and Ireland, you feel overwhelmed, don't you?" "Yes," the interviewer replied. "Well," he said, "we feel the same if not more, but there is one difference." "What difference?" the interviewer asked.

To which the physician responded, "You can't lose hope as long as you are making friends."

The attitude of both the Vietnamese father and daughter as well as this physician helped remove the "psychological cataracts" from my eyes and replace them with an outlook of gratitude and hope. It made me appreciate more deeply than ever before a truth that has held fast for me while working with people going through trauma and during my own tough times: *It is not the amount of darkness in the world or even in ourselves that matters; it is how we stand in that darkness.*

I remember how David Steindl-Rast, who is known for his work on gratefulness and mindfulness, reported that during a war, he recognized that when he would come out of a bunker where he hid for shelter and see a patch of grass, it seemed greener to him than any grass he had ever seen before. Was it really greener? Or, was his appreciation for life much more in his mind's eye? Later, he was to reflect on this and other experiences in his life and recognize that most of us leave the house each day with a list, and on that list is what we will be grateful for. He suggested throwing away the list so we could be open to be grateful for everything in possibly new ways.

The mini-culture we refer to as "family" or "close friends" have values, likes, and dislikes, as well as obvious views and unexamined prejudices. As we interact with them, our direct appreciation of life may become dulled. Psychological cataracts form through habitual contact with the way others view life. When this happens we slowly, without discerning it, fail to see the world afresh any longer.

There are times in life, such as adolescence, when we get glimpses of this perceptual imprisonment and seek to break out. But as with an effort at escape, the risk is often taken in such a dramatic or unusual way that like a boomerang, it only serves to come back to hurt, rather than free, us.

So what is the answer? How can we both see ourselves and our lives clearly but not become rash in our attempts to remove what is currently making our views opaque? The answer is in the simplicity and pacing of self-knowledge and new actions that result from tranquility gained from periods of mindfulness, as well as honing other psychological virtues that arise out of a sense of intrigue about, and commitment to, seeing things clearly.

In the words of counselor, Buddhist guide, and author of the classic work, *Zen Therapy*, David Brazier, "Tranquility erodes the mind's conditioning. Conditioning makes us compulsive."

Tenacity, patience, and humility are essential as well—especially when we are challenged to see things we might want to avoid. A very talented and committed colleague of mine who wound up in jail because of financial improprieties, attested to this beautifully by writing the following:

> During my time here, I have become a real devotee of crossword puzzles, especially those in the *New York Times*. Before, I was always "too busy for puzzles," except the ones that I wrought! Anyway, I learned early on that crossword puzzles in general, and specifically in the *Times*, progress in difficulty as the week passes. So, Monday was easy, even in the beginning. At this point, I can do through Thursday, unassisted; but, Friday to Sunday takes more time and a thesaurus, dictionary, and "peeks" at the solutions that are subsequently published.
>
> There's a temptation to want to skip the Friday–Sunday and leap ahead to Monday–Thursday. I've seen in this an interesting allegory to my life. It's tempting to want to "skip ahead" and pass the more difficult chapters. Sometimes, even leaving them "undone" is (or seems) easier. I want the easy ones! So, here—for now—I am stuck in the hard part—my little "long weekend." I have to stick with it, knowing that a Monday—an easier time—awaits me.

The puzzles have also helped me in other ways. They require more patience with myself and the puzzle. Sometimes putting it down for a day brings clarity. The next day, I know the answer right away, and I wonder why it eluded me the day before. I have learned that I can think too hard sometimes. The puzzles also make me focus; I can't multitask. Finally, crossword puzzles are humbling. I am stretched *and* I must acknowledge that I don't know everything—not nearly so. I need to rely on the thesaurus, the dictionary, and even the solutions that are, inevitably printed, I need to rely on . . . friends . . . too.

Removing the psychological cataracts on our own will be difficult. Also, as recognized by my colleague in the preceding statement, this could mean that all of us, including (maybe *especially*) those who are professional helpers and healers, may need to turn to someone wiser for help. The mentorship we seek may come from a book we have read or even a movie we have seen where the characters, true or fictional, provide us with some words that turn into lifelines offering new openness, a spirit of unlearning, and gratitude. We must realize, however, that at certain turning points in our lives, we may need to turn to an actual physical mentor for support. And an immediate obvious question arises: What would such a person look like for us?

FIVE

PROFILE OF A FUTURE MENTOR

If you want to go fast, go alone.
If you want to go far, go together.
—CAMEROONIAN PROVERB

Anumber of years ago, I was sitting in a colleague's office chatting with him about an article that was published in the *New Yorker* magazine. He was my best friend and I thoroughly enjoyed discussing issues with him that we both found intriguing. It led to wonderful conversations and insights. The article in question was on psychoanalysis, and we both found it fascinating and, at times, humorous. But then came a surprising turn of events. There was a period of silence in which we were obviously reflecting on both the article and our conversation up to this point, and then my friend began to share both his thoughts and feelings in a way I hadn't heard before.

"You know, once I finished reading the article, I actually filled up emotionally and cried a bit."

This response certainly caught me off guard; not simply because of its content but also because of how he shared it.

I could see he was visibly emotional now as he revealed to me that something had happened in his reading of the article that hadn't struck me in the same way. So I waited and allowed him to amplify on his initial comment, which I knew he would.

Once he seemed to get hold of himself, he added, "When the writer shared his feelings about the death of his analyst, I thought of my own losses. But what I think was most poignant for me was how it reminded me that I had not received the mentoring I felt I needed, or at least *desired* in my life."

He went on to say, "I've been in my own personal psychotherapy. I had been clinically supervised on my cases. Yet I felt what I lacked was a wisdom figure, someone with whom to share my hopes, desires, and life in a natural way."

His words at that moment brought me back to a fortuitous event in my own life. I had been attending a lecture on the contemplative, forward thinker and writer, Thomas Merton. One of the two persons delivering the presentation, Flavian Burns, struck me as the type of mentor I had been looking for over a period of years. In the way he was handling questions and comments, I could see that he was welcoming, bright, a true listener, and not someone pushing an individual agenda of his own. The thought occurred to me, "Since I walked with others in darkness, should I not also have someone who would walk with me on a regular basis, not simply when I felt in crisis myself. I wonder if someone as prominent as Flavian Burns would consider being a mentor to me?"

The thought didn't leave me for days, so I took this as a sign to take action on it. I wrote him, telling him a bit about myself, and asking if he would consider meeting with me for mentoring. He responded almost immediately with an invitation to come and speak with him about it. I did, it went well, and the mentoring relationship lasted until his death.

My friend's reaction and my opportunity to act are actually not surprising today. Because of the mobility of society, the absence of senior, wise family members, and the lack of structured mentoring in most professional and business settings, many people feel deeply the need for a welcoming ear, guidance, and some encouragement in today's anxious world. This absence can be sensed dramatically as in the case of minimalist poet, Robert Lax who wrote: "I feel sure that what held me about Bramacari was not so much his ideas . . . but his personality, and the kind of civilization—the kind of planet—he came from . . . as though I had always felt there must be that kind of planet somewhere and I was glad to see a representative of it come our way at last."

Receiving such mentoring can also lead to being in the position of returning the favor to others, if asked. In the case of Lax, there were many others who turned to him as he entered the latter part of his life on the isle of Patmos. In one book on his conversations with Lax (*The Way of the Dreamcatcher*), Steve Georgiou writes, "Already in my thirties, I was at a point of transition and sought a role model who could teach me how to age well, and not grow 'old.' I needed a guide, a sage to help me in my soul searching or at least give me the confidence that a harmonic sense of balance in this life could be personally attained and shared with others." The fact that this did occur for Georgiou is marked at the end of the book when he concludes, "I remember how after spending long evenings with Lax, I would leave the hermitage and feel as though I had landed on earth for the first time."

In a more recent, more comprehensive book on the life of Lax entitled *Pure Act*, the author, Michael McGregor, sets the stage for his eventual meeting with and being mentored by Lax—who was once referred to as the "laughing Buddha" by Beat poet, Jack Kerouac—by sharing his dilemma about being a deeply compassionate, yet lost individual at the time.

I'd gone to Europe that year, 1985, because I had questions. Huge questions. Seemingly unanswerable questions. They were questions about how to live in a world full of pain and violence and need. A world in which few people seemed to think about the way they lived and its effect on others. For the past three years I'd been writing about poverty, oppression, and illness in the world's poorest countries. I'd interviewed subsistence farmers in remote areas of Bangladesh, Khmer Rouge refugees on the borders of Cambodia, and children in Nepal and India crippled by diseases long eradicated from developed nations. In a camp surrounded by barb-wire, I'd listened to a beautiful Vietnamese refugee describe repeated rapes by Thai

pirates. I didn't know what to do with her tears, or with
the endless lines of homeless people on Calcutta's streets,
or with the orphan girl who took my hand and squeezed
it tightly in Thailand, as if a touch could make up for the
sight she'd lost to disease . . . The main question that tortured me was this: What should I be doing? How should
I be living? Just writing about misery and efforts to allevi-
ate it didn't seem enough.

Both Georgiou and McGregor were bringing their life
experiences to Lax, in this case, in the hopes of making greater
sense of their stories than they could on their own. They were
seeking a form of wisdom that would allow them, in turn, to
continue to share with others in need—possibly on a deeper
level—what they had and would learn.

PROFILE OF A MENTOR

A seasoned psychiatrist was once asked by his wife why he visited a mentor every six weeks, after all, she said to him, he
was a psychiatrist. His response was simple: "Where he is, is
where I want to be. In that place of sanity." Yet we have long
known that such mentors are not easy to find. Long ago, it even
prompted psychiatrist Carl Jung to ask, "Where are the wise
and wonderful persons of old who did not merely talk about
life but actually lived it?"

Given this, in looking for a mentor when I first sought ongoing mentoring, I needed to develop at least a vague profile for what I might be looking for and what traits would be helpful for this person to have. This would also mature more clearly in my own mind the approach I should take as a mentor to others.

Finally, although I thought finding all these traits or gifts in one person might not be possible, I realized my ideal mentor would have the following abilities:

- Ask questions that invigorate my thinking to see both possibility and challenge in new ways.
- Help me return to the clatter and commotion of my life a little differently with a way of living with humility and dignity in this transient, anxious world.
- Demonstrate a faith in me rather than asking me to have faith in him or her.
- Be in touch with a truth that seemed bigger than the truths I was living by.
- Be as sincere as I hoped I was.
- Recognize that I was looking for some meaning, peace, and joy as well as to understand myself a bit better than all my training and experience had offered me up to this point.
- Help me see more clearly that the mentoring process isn't simply my listening to a mentor so carefully that I would know everything the mentor did, but instead through listening with a sense of true openness, I might find a way to mature what I already have within me.

- Offer me the "psychological room" to be myself.
- Encourage a sense of wonder and awe in me about being who I am now and who I can be as I turn the corner of the different phases in my life and work.
- Stand with me in the darkness until I found a new perspective and deeper sense of self that might not have been possible had the difficulties not appeared in the first place.
- Be practical and mindful of the realities of life but not captured by them.
- Share his or her *charism* or primary psychological gift in a way that might allow me to find and fathom mine more deeply than before.
- Provide guidance without giving answers; offer support but not remove my own independence and faith in myself to discover an approach that would be most suitable given my own personality and circumstances.

In preparing this list, I realized even more that what all of us need to understand most about mentors is their ability to welcome us in ways that allow us the greatest freedom to be *ourselves*. This is especially so when we feel we are most ready to *unlearn* what we are holding onto that is not helpful and open ourselves to new wisdom that would empower us during the next phase of our lives.

Too often, the people around us, even the ones we consider wise, have agendas, need a level of affirmation, want to succeed, and are not empty enough to truly be helpful. As Jack Kornfield in his encouraging work with the humorous title, *After the Ecstasy, the Laundry*, notes: "The understanding of emptiness [genuine openness, acceptance, freedom] is contagious. It appears we can catch it from one another. We know that when a sad or angry person enters a room, we too often enter sadness or anger. It shouldn't surprise us then, that the presence of a teacher who is empty, open, awake can have a powerful effect on another person especially if that person is ripe."

I remember once seeing an anonymously written quote, "A friend knows the song in your heart, and can sing it back to you when you have forgotten how it goes." If ever this were true, it is the case with respect to receiving and offering mentoring when true emptiness is present. The impact is palpable. As Mitch Albom, in his bestselling book, *Tuesdays with Morrie*, recognized, "When I visited Morrie I liked myself better when I was there.

During my times with my own mentor as we often walked along the Shenandoah River, my sense was the world was a better place and my life in it was an honor. Even though it has been more than ten years since my time with him, I can still feel those moments of friendship. Author Henry James once proclaimed, "A teacher affects eternity, he can never tell where his influence stops." This is how I still feel about my own mentor and is a standard for my own time sitting with others both in the darkness and at times of great joy in their lives. The atmosphere rather than the lessons remain. The music of mentoring more than the lyrics still inspire me to believe in possibility at each stage of life. Not the possibility that I might wish but that which is offered if we have the eyes to see.

With respect to therapists (and I think we can say this of mentors even more) Jeffrey Kottler in his classic work for clinicians, *On Being a Therapist*, notes the following:

> Lock a person, any person, in a room alone with Sigmund Freud, Carl Rogers, Fritz Perls, Albert Ellis, or any formidable personality, and several hours later he will come out different. It is not what the therapist does that is important but rather who she is. A therapist who is vibrant, inspirational, charismatic, who is sincere, loving, and nurturing, who is wise, confident, and self-disciplined will have a dramatic impact by the sheer force and power of her essence. . . .
>
> The first and foremost element of change, then is the therapist's presence—his excitement, enthusiasm, and the power of his personality . . . The therapist enters the relationship with clarity, openness, and serenity and comes fully prepared to encounter a soul in torment. The client comes prepared with his own expectations for a mentor, a doctor, a friend, or a wizard.

That is why it is important that a mentor enable a healthy psychological environment to flourish by possessing many of the preceding traits. They contribute to a sense that something is happening in the encounter, although we might not know it at the time. More than once I would drive away from my own mentoring session and wonder whether anything had happened. I would question something said or a comment made as being unrealistic. Then, I would drive a bit further, and it would hit me as to what was there for me. The philosopher Sartre's words, "To live well is both difficult and possible" would be given new life in the concrete encounters and challenges that I was called to meet in a different way or, even at a more basic level, recognize possibly for the first time in a helpful way.

Much of the time we fail to either find a mentor or use the gifts of this person properly because we expect answers. A good mentor will resist this pull from us. Shunryu Suzuki, a Buddhist guide, once said, "If I give you an answer you'll think you understand." Merton echoed this sentiment in saying, "No one can give you a map. Your terrain is unique. Just some guidance and courage on how to handle the terrain."

Instead, the wise friend in our lives will help us live with the questions, *our* questions, possibly until they can get big enough or be the right ones for us to address. Their gift to us in such instances is to be willing to model a psychological virtue that is not valued much in today's world. Once again, here are the guiding words of Rilke to the young poet who was seeking his wise presence through their correspondence:

> I want to beg you, as much as I can, dear sir, to be patient toward all that is unsolved in your heart and to try to love the questions themselves, like locked rooms and like books

that are written in a foreign tongue. Do not now seek the answers, which cannot be given you because you would not be able to live them. And the point is to live everything. Live the questions now. Perhaps you will gradually, without noticing it, live along some distant day into the answers.

Or in the words of a hermit in the desert when approached by a young man who was speaking about things he only knew about and had not tried, and possibly failed at, doing himself, "You have not found a boat, or put your oar in it, and you haven't even sailed, but you seem to have arrived in the city already! Well, do your work first; then you will come to the point you are talking about now."

SOME FINAL THOUGHTS ON RECEIVING MENTORING

In the beginning of his book, *The Life You Save May Be Your Own*, Paul Elie places four photographs of the authors he is going to discuss for the remainder of the work. He then comments, "In the photographs, they don't look like people who might make you want to change your life." He then goes on to portray them as writers who "make their readers yearn to go and do likewise."

For us to "go and do likewise" through receiving mentoring, we need to seek out someone who might stand with us at crucial points in our lives. However, even if we are success-ful in finding someone, the journey does not end there. As Sogyal Rinpoche notes in his book *The Tibetan Book of Living and Dying*, "One of the greatest things to model is being a student all your life of the great masters." However, he goes on to caution, "You may have the karma [good fortune] to find a teacher, but you must then create the karma to follow your teacher."

This is done by listening to the verbal feedback, noting the nonverbal reactions, and resolving to follow what you learn by putting this new wisdom into practice in ways that *you* feel appropriate and relevant in your life. You have the ownership of your narrative. In the end, in mentoring, as in all wisdom relationships, there must be a sense that you are the student, that you have the openness and inner space to welcome new knowledge (and a feeling of uncomfortableness or irritability is a sign it isn't), and that determined prac-tice of new insights in your own behavior is undertaken and never neglected.

Discouragement is always a factor. Anytime real change is desired or a new way of relating to self and others is sought, there is a temptation to pull back. Author Andrew Harvey related in his work, *Journey in Ladakh*, that he shared with a com-panion, "It is hard at this time to believe in any help." Often therapists and other helpers especially can feel this because they have helped others and feel when they are depressed that the helping process may be simply all techniques or even "tricks." Yet to Harvey's surprise, the person he shared this with responded by saying something all of us should remember when we are living within a sense of darkness: "That is because you have not found out where help is." Bringing to greater clarity what we are looking for in a mentor is the first step in finding such needed help.

SIX

SIMPLICITY OF SERIOUS SELF-CARE

What if life is like a plane and you miss it?
—WALKER PERCY

*I think that any man who watches three football
games in a row should be declared legally dead.*
—ERMA BOMBECK

If we are open to receiving wisdom and key life lessons from daily encounters, such wisdom may come from people and at times when we least expect it. Such was the case with me in terms of looking at incorporating self-care in simple, realistic ways. This is so important because persons who care for others are often the worst at taking care of themselves. The preceding usual funny-but-true words by Erma Bombeck note that many of us involved in providing care for others surprisingly seem to have no "menu" of activities and steps to take care of ourselves. As a result, we simply exist on whatever psychological or spiritual food that happens to be conveniently available. Consequently, such renewing factors as meditation, interaction with friends, and time by ourselves, turn into luxuries rather than necessary, planned psychological refreshment.

The turning point for me in realizing this came when I was only in my thirties. I was living in West Chester, Pennsylvania, teaching at Bryn Mawr College's Graduate School of Social Work and Social Research. I also had a clinical practice in Rittenhouse Square in Philadelphia, making rounds on Sunday at a hospital in Lancaster, Pennsylvania, and in the process of all these activities . . . quickly burning out myself!

Then, I received a call from an old friend from New York City. I was the best man at his wedding and when I relocated, he moved, and slowly we lost touch. It had been more than ten years since we had a meaningful conversation. I was thrilled to hear his voice and recognized it in an instant. You could tell that he was also pleased that we were able to reconnect. He opened the conversation by asking me how I was doing and what I was up to at work. In response, I enthusiastically shared all that I was involved in—not only as a university professor and author but especially in my consultancy and presentations to helping and healing professionals on resilience. I told him this is a work I truly love because it puts me in touch with leaders and novices in such areas as psychology, psychiatry, social work, counseling, ministry, education, medicine, and nursing. I loved it, but the intensity of work with helpers under great stress themselves that included long hours, frequent travel to other countries, and particularly my own concern about the impact I was having were all taking a real toll on me.

Finally, after sharing with him for a while what was happening in my life, I asked him, "Well, how are you doing, Fred?" In response, he said almost matter of factly, "Well, actually Bob, I'm dying."

Since we were only in our thirties at the time and he was such a lively force—even then while he was speaking with me—he caught me completely off guard, and I said in an incredulous voice, "You're dying? What do you mean, 'you're dying?'"

"Well, Bob, I have something called 'astrocytoma,' a rare form of brain cancer. My mother thinks I am going to experience a miracle, but you know when you are dying, and I'm dying, Bob."

It took me a while to digest this, so we were both quiet for some time, and then finally I asked, "Where are you calling from Fred?" He responded, "Misericordia Hospital in Philadelphia."

I was surprised. He wasn't in New York City. He was actually near me for some reason. So I said, "Misericordia Hospital? Why you are only about forty minutes from where I live. Would you like me to visit?"

"Would it be a big deal?" he asked. "No. Not at all," I told him.

"Well, when are you coming?"

"*Right now,*" I responded with emphasis.

I went downstairs, quickly briefed my wife on the situation, told her I'd be gone for several hours, hopped in the car, and drove into Philadelphia.

After I arrived and was in the room for a few moments, I realized that even though he was convinced he was dying, he was still the same outrageous guy who lived up the street from me in Queens, New York City. As a result, I knew he would expect me not to be any different with him given his situation. I must have had this firmly planted in my mind, because when I asked him what his symptoms were and he told me he had two particularly irritating ones—he couldn't hold his water so he had to wear a diaper, and he had lost his short-term memory so he couldn't remember anything at all about the two weeks he had already been here in the hospital—I responded, "Well, that loss of memory is tragic!" In response, he looked puzzled and asked, "Why is my loss of memory of what has happened here tragic?" To which I quickly responded, "Because you don't remember me sitting here by your bed for six hours each day for the past couple of weeks."

For a moment he looked startled and then said something to me with such colorful language that I still laugh thinking about it. My comment accomplished what I felt was needed at that moment. He had probably been faced with friends and family who were so caught up in the tension and severity of the situation that they weren't of much help to him. I could see from his facial expression and more relaxed demeanor in bed that he knew he could chat freely with an old friend who he wouldn't have to reassure, as is the case with many people when they are faced with someone in their interpersonal circle going through a serious, traumatic situation as Fred was.

Once we had settled in and got caught up to date on his condition and both our lives since we had last seen each other, he asked me a question that I first thought was a simple throwaway inquiry: "Well, what have you been doing that has been *especially* important over the past several years?" Since during both the phone call and the first hour of our visit we had already gone into depth about what had been happening, I assumed he was referring to key accomplishments that I was proud of and so I began listing them.

He waved a hand of dismay at me and quickly let me know I wasn't responding to what he was interested in and told me. "No. No. Not that stuff. The *important* stuff."

"I am not sure what you are referring to then, Fred?"

"Bob, the important stuff." He said these four words slowly, as if he were speaking to someone who spoke English as a second language and needed time to translate in his mind what was being communicated before answering it. Then, he started to tick off a number of questions:

> Tell me about the quiet walks you take by yourself each day.
>
> What museums do you belong to?
>
> What books have you read and movies have you seen recently?
>
> Where do you go fishing?

Tell me about your circle of friends and what are their psychological voices they provide for you so you don't go astray?

You know, the *important* stuff.

I must admit, I sat there stunned. Here was someone who was dying and soon according to his sense of things would no longer be able to enjoy life as I should be doing, and he was teaching me about living, self-care, and not forgetting to live life to the fullest while it was there. Later on, I would think back to this encounter when I read the words in a novel by physician and author Walker Percy where the question is posed, "What if life is like a plane and you miss it?"

I would also think again and again what he had asked about my circle of friends. Who was in it? What different voices did they offer me so my life would be balanced? And would I hear comments from them that were appropriately challenging, encouraging, inspirational, and humorous? Later I would describe such friends in my writings and presentations as the *prophet* who asked "What voices are guiding you in life that you might not be aware of?"; the *cheerleader* who would be sympathetic and on my side no matter what I had done; the *harasser or teaser* who would help me recognize that on the way to taking seriously what was truly important in life, I had taken a detour and taken myself too seriously instead; and, finally, the *inspirational friend* who called me to be all that I could be without embarrassing me that I was psychologically where I was at that moment.

But it was his final question with respect to what he was asking me that struck me the most. After I spoke about the renewing and fun things I was involved in as well as the people that gave me life in different enriching ways, he said, "I did want to ask you one more thing."

"What is it, Fred?"

"You don't have to answer it if you don't want."

I asked again, "What is it, Fred?"

"If I weren't dying, I wouldn't ask."

Finally, I leaned back in my seat and asked, "What is it?"

"Well, as I mentioned, I am dying, but I'm not afraid."

"You're not?" I asked.

"No. But I feel that shortly I will be entering a large silence, and I remember that you faithfully take time out each morning in silence and solitude and wrapped in gratitude. If you could tell me what happens in your periods of silence, I think it would help me die."

As he had intimated, he did die several months after that, and I will never forget this interaction. It reminded me more forcefully than anything else that I needed to develop a self-care program for myself that was realistic, touched all aspects of my life, was well thought out, and immediately implemented in some way.

I began to realize that even if exercise only involved a quiet walk each day, I would benefit. Too often, the grayness I and others feel after work is not the result of something untoward happening during the day but the poor air circulation in some of the buildings and offices in which we work. A short walk each day would help with this.

I could also think more intentionally about the food I was eating to ensure that I wasn't just grabbing whatever was around.

I needed to think through who was in my circle of friends and what different "voices" were present to help me remain encouraged, awake, flexible, and hopeful.

And finally, in preparing a self-care program for myself that touched all the bases, I needed to ensure that I had quiet time to renew, reflect, adjust, be in touch with myself, and simply breathe rather than taking in air and life in gulps.

Time and again, I would fall back into my old patterns of rushing through life to do all those "important things," feeling that this was only practical, natural, and necessary. Then, as it often did, life would provide a wake-up call, and I remembered hearing about an old rabbi who was asked what he had learned during his long tenure at his shul. He reflected for a bit and then said that he had found few people who were irresponsible. Instead, he encountered persons who were constantly busy and, if it weren't for the Sabbath would fail to truly enjoy and know to be grateful for the life with which they were gifted.

After hearing this, when I had a patient cancel her therapy appointment, I took the time for someone as equally impor-tant: *me.* I took out a sheet of paper and began to prepare what I hoped would be both a realistic, creative, and exten-sive list of elements that I should consider in my self-care protocol. I did this not simply so I could then put it into my desk drawer and feel I had accomplished something. I did it to sensitize myself to the reality that if I didn't take care of myself, no one else would. If I waited to live my life later, it would never happen.

What surprised me was that the list didn't seem radical but was still comprehensive enough to make me ask myself why I don't enjoy these activities more in my life. When did I expect to have the space to enjoy and nurture myself—just before I die? As I pull out the list for review as I have done so many times before, some of the following entries strike me:

- Taking quiet walks
- Finding crumbs of alonetime so I can lean back and reflect quietly by myself
- Reading for ten minutes or so a novel or biography of some-one who would inspire me
- Enjoying a conversation in person, over the phone, or via email with a friend
- Listening to some old music that I used to enjoy but have not listened to recently
- Visiting a local park or museum
- Stopping in at a bookstore to browse and have a latté
- Reading poetry out loud
- Sitting propped up in bed to watch the morning news

- Planting a small garden with both perennials and annuals, so I could have the fun of seeing what I have put in come back to life and decorate the garden with new ideas as well
- Taking a walk through town during lunchtime
- Journaling at the end of the day on what happened (the objective) and what I felt about it (the subjective) so I could learn a bit more about myself

Once again, I was to realize that in acting on this list, it was not simply about me:

> One of the greatest gifts I could share with others was a sense of my own peace, a healthy perspective, and as resilient a lifestyle as possible . . . but I could not share what I didn't have.

As I drove home after visiting my friend Fred, and at later points in life, I also appreciated even more that one of the key psychological fruits of self-care, which included quiet time and good friendship, is a fuller appreciation of who I was becoming through the different situations and developing times of my life. Such a greater awareness, however, would take closer attention. All of us, no matter whether we are professionals in the helping and healing arenas or are simply giving people trying to be present to our families and friends in good ways, need to take special stock of ourselves as we move through the phases of our own life.

In my time with myself—as well as in providing psychotherapy, mentoring, and supervision to clinicians and others in the helping profession—I found that framing these periods or phases, as three "inner journeys" for myself and others was helpful. How I myself and other people navigated them, especially the third journey, would indeed be telling—not only in how they worked with others but also how they would enjoy and benefit from their own experience of life. Moreover, one of the surprising elements in self-reflection and in guiding others was a strength or virtue that few of us seem to appreciate and honor sufficiently: *ordinariness*.

SEVEN

Beginning the Three Essential Inner Journeys: Honoring and Fathoming

When it is clear—if I have eyes to see—that the life I am living is not the same as the life that wants to live in me . . . I [start] to understand that it is indeed possible to live a life other than one's own . . . I had simply found a "noble" way to live a life that was not my own, a life spent imitating heroes instead of listening to my heart.

—Parker Palmer, *Let Your Life Speak*

In an anecdotal comment about how a prisoner of war was able to survive his time in captivity, he was described as a simple man who knew who he was. The interrogations did not work to dissemble his psychological state because he did not either over or under emphasize who he was. He was at peace with who he was. He was . . . *ordinary*. Having this strength or virtue when we care for others as professionals or with those in our family or circle of friends is important not only to us but to those we serve. Unfortunately, it is often not as appreciated as it could be.

Recognizing this, psychologist and spiritual writer Henri Nouwen, in a reflection on compassion in his book, *Reaching Out*, writes:

> When we think back to the places where we felt most at home, we quickly see that it was where our hosts gave us the precious freedom to come and go on our own terms and did not claim us for their own needs. Only in a free space can re-creation take place and new life be found. The real host is one who offers that space where we do not have to be afraid and where we can listen to our own inner voices and find our own personal way of being human. But to be such a host we have to first of all be at home in our own house.

As professional helpers and healers would tell us, to be at home in this way takes some attention and the right kind of effort. The question, "Why do I choose to help people?" naturally leads to the one, "How can I best help others?" Yet, as important as both of these questions are, whether I am a professional or am simply reaching out to family, friends, and coworkers, the underlying more important question that I must face is *"Who* am I as the helper and how comfortable am I within my own skin?" This question also becomes challenging when we realize that it cannot be answered once and for all. As we change, so do our gifts, potential, and sense of self.

Most psychotherapists go through their own therapy as a way of understanding both this process of treatment and to take greater stock of themselves as people. Since I have worked with healing and helping professionals for many years, I have also noted that persons in training or in the early years of practicing medicine, social work, education, and ministry also often seek out a form of "growth therapy." In doing this, they are not seeking to be "repaired" so much as to recognize at certain points in life who they have become, who they are called to be at that point, and what it will take to flow with their lives more fully.

Bantu tribespeople, it is said, sneak into the room of their children as they sleep and whisper into their ears, "Become what you are." Yet, as we all recognize, in contemporary life, this is easier said than done. As poet e. e. cummings once noted, "To be nobody but yourself in a world which is trying to make you everyone else is worth fighting for . . . and never stop fighting." This is a message not only for ourselves but one to share with others as well.

A number of years ago a priest who worked in a large Midwestern parish recognized that although he was assigned to this work, he also felt a real call to work with the poor. And so, at night when his work was done and he had finished dinner, he would go down to the basement kitchen and make sandwiches for the homeless. He then took a little cart, filled it with the food, and walked through a poorer part of town where there were many street people. Because he felt this was a vocation and a natural extension of who he was, he wasn't concerned about the success or impact of his work or how people responded. Some would simply throw away the sandwiches he gave them and ask for money for drink instead. Others would spit at him, while still others would thank him for thinking of them. None of their responses really seemed to matter. He felt it was *his* work to reach out in this way, no matter what the results or reactions.

Eventually, somehow the newspapers got wind of his work and publicized it. In response, people started sending him money. Yet, instead of caring about the newfound fame or keeping the money, he returned the donations with a one-line message: "Make your own damn sandwiches." To his mind, more important than their supporting his work, was the call to discover and respond to their *own* calls in life.

We can also see this reality being appreciated by the following two authors. Poet Rainer Maria Rilke, author of the powerful guidance contained in *Letters to a Young Poet*, was amazed by fellow poet Stefan George's focus solely on the quality of his work—not the pursuit of success in others' eyes. He appreciated his ability to be faithful to his work without needing recognition. Writer Flannery O'Connor, recognizing this to be so, also once quipped, "Fame is something you have in common with Miss Watermelon 1955."

When we live life in an egotistical cocoon marked only by self-concern and self-protection, we miss so much of the experience of life. In a similar vein, it is also easy to become merely "a responder" to the desires and needs of those around us. One colleague of mine wore so many masks I didn't think she really knew who she was anymore or, at times, became improbable even to herself.

Most people—including many helpers and healers— believe that there are overarching ways to "call" people to develop themselves so they can enjoy their lives and more freely share their gifts with others even when they, themselves, are experiencing tough times. In other words, as some would term it: to live a rewarding life that results from healthy self-care and gracious compassion.

To accomplish this, I have found in my own work with professionals in the healing and helping arena, as well as others who turn to me for therapy or mentoring, that it is important to make the most of three essential psychological journeys:

1. *Honor* a central sense of self.
2. *Fathom* what other gifts we might have which need further attention, exploration and development.
3. *Release* what ego investment we have in our identity at a certain point so as to experience greater freedom during the generative period of our late adulthood.

The *first journey* (honoring self) is an obvious, but admittedly not easy one. It is the process during childhood, adolescence, and young adulthood of finding out who you really are. In simple terms, it is the search for true self-appreciation or self-understanding. This is normally accomplished through reflection, wholesome feedback from others, and any other efforts that result in developing a well-rounded sense of self.

While this, of course, involves our willingness to see our "growing edges"—those areas where we fall short, unreflectively become defensive, or seem unaware of their negative impact on us and others—the most captivating part of this phase of our journey is to truly appreciate our primary gift or notable signature strength. When we are able to do this, we can actually feel inwardly stronger and use this gift to help uncover and diminish those areas of our personality and style that seem to trip us up at times. The goal is to appreciate our uniqueness without becoming overly self-conscious or too self-involved. Self-examination without self-absorption is not easy. Yet, it is essential that we understand, honor, and befriend our personality if we are to enjoy and share our lives. As Pema Chödrön, author of *When Things Fall Apart*, learned from a mentor, "When you make good friends with yourself, your situation will become more friendly too."

The *second journey* is a bit more nuanced than the first. It is part of the maturing process from young to middle adulthood and generally involves a psychological pruning that many people unfortunately never undertake or even know about. If the first call's goal is to move forward and actualize our central *charism*, gift, or signature strength, then the second one is to psychologically take a few steps back to see how we can balance our primary approach to life so that it can become even more effective. So, those of us who are quite passionate, for instance, might find we must also be gentler than in the past or our style will sometimes come across as intrusive or as "taking up too much space" in the interpersonal room where we are at any given time.

If the person is a listener to whom people enjoy coming to share their journeys, there are times when this person must balance out this welcoming stance with a more assertive one. Otherwise, this wonderful listening spirit will merely become a diffident one marked by a lack of involvement, rather than a really welcoming spirit. In finding and employing this balancing gift, we will find as we are attentive to it that it is also a portal to discovering lesser noted signature strengths in ourselves as well.

The *third and final journey* involves letting go or releasing. During middle to late adulthood, when this process seems developmentally appropriate for most people who have been actively compassionate, we must confront the following central question: "How can I release or let go of being centered on my primary gift as I was when I was younger (e.g., in my case, "passion") and instead center myself on the primary balancing strength that can be discovered and developed in my second journey?" So, if one, as in the case of myself, is known for his or her passion, now the desire is to really try to be most aware of and first and foremost share the gift of gentleness instead.

External circumstances and our inner world change at different junctures in life. Being attuned to these periods and offering them respect and the right type of attention can make all the difference. When this doesn't happen, it can be quite obvious. When teenage rebellion or risk-taking as a way to exert a level of independence and experiment with different identities doesn't occur, it may show up later in life with disastrous results. If during middle age, the crisis of change is not negotiated, then immaturity and acting out can result.

Our narrative is always undergoing the possibility of development, which may cause us concern. In *High Tide in Tucson*, Barbara Kingsolver talks about this in a very captivating way. She writes, "Everyone of us is called upon, probably many times to start a new life. A frightening diagnosis, a marriage, a move, loss of a job or a limb or a loved one, a graduation, bringing a new baby home: it's impossible to think at first how this all will be possible."

At such junctures, it is easy to give up and give in to our temptation to freeze time on the one hand. On the other hand, we can look at where we are and hope to go next. We can see how our motives and ideas have progressed and where we are holding on. To accomplish this, as we move through each stage in life, we ask ourselves a series of questions, which might include the following:

- What would it take for me to be able to make the most of this stage I am in?
- Who would be good mentors for me in this stage of life?
- What would give me joy both personally and professionally, as this would result in me maximizing my life and naturally lead me to share it with others?

- What skills do I need and how can I be confident in them rather than either fall prey to extreme doubt or inordinate self-confidence?
- How can I catch myself when I am just going through the motions in life so I can revisit my original passion and see what is blocking me from enjoying and deepening my life?
- In what ways can I share the fruits of the preceding efforts?

When these questions are asked with the right spirit, they can be transformative, because informally answering them or ones like them provide a flow for an ongoing way to approach life. Minimalist poet Robert Lax, in a note to his artist friend, Nancy Goldring describes this beautifully.

not
so
much
finding
a
path
in
the
woods
as
find
ing
a

rhythm

to

walk

in

As was previously noted, Lax found such a rhythm in meeting a person from India by the name of Brahmachari and says,
"I feel sure that what held me about him was not so much his
ideas . . . but his personality, and the kind of civilization—the
kind of planet—he came from . . . as though I had always felt
there must be that kind of planet somewhere and I was glad to
see a representative of it come our way at last."

Such a spirit involves avoiding the psychological dead ends
of arrogance, ignorance, or discouragement. In the case of *arrogance*, we give the environment too much credit and fail to see
our own role in making our way in life. This may involve projecting blame onto others or feeling only a miracle or winning
the psychological lottery by meeting just the right person or
possessing a perfect job will do the trick.

In the case of ignorance, on the trail to self-discovery, we
take a detour onto the path of self-blame. In such instances,
we berate ourselves for past mistakes or current failures. This
accomplishes nothing, because behavior in yourself that you
wince at will turn into behavior that you wink at. You can't
constantly look at yourself in a negative way and expect to
achieve balanced insights or feel the strength of your own gifts
in a way that allows you to move ahead.

The final cul-de-sac is *discouragement*. We begin to feel this emotion because you, or someone else, has paced you too quickly or you expect too much, too quickly. When this happens, as French philosopher Alain writes, "You don't need to be a sorcerer to cast a spell over yourself by saying, 'This is how I am I can do nothing about it.'" Unfortunately, this final turning back can happen at the very moment where new psychological self-understanding and depth may be in the offing. As one Zen master said to a practitioner who was ready to give up on mindfulness practices, "You try and you fail. You try and you fail again and then eventually you go deeper." One of the ways we can go "deeper" is by attending to each of these three phases or journeys in our life beginning with the sense of "honoring" of who we truly are.

HONORING

William James, philosopher and father of American psychology, once noted, "I have often thought that the best way to define a man's character would be to seek out the particular mental or moral attitude in which, when it came upon him, he felt himself most deeply and intensely active and alive. At such moments there is a voice inside which speaks and says: 'This is the real me!'" Yet, if we are not sensitive to this voice, then as George Orwell once noted, "You wear a mask, and your face grows to fit it."

During childhood, up to and through adolescence until young adulthood, the goal for many—no matter how they might frame it—is to find oneself rather than simply copy models that are offered for consideration by family, friends, and society at large.

What are we honoring? It is the identity given to us not by our parents, not by society but inherent in us. The question faced in this first journey is "What is my true *charism*, my true 'word,' my true 'name' or purpose on this earth?" I don't think we realize how important it is to know this.

In his book *So Long, See You Tomorrow*, William Maxwell makes it clear in the following story:

A lighthouse keeper who worked on a rocky stretch of coastline received his new supply of oil once a month to keep his light burning. Not being far from shore, he had frequent guests. One night a woman from the village begged some oil to keep her family warm. Another time a father asked for some to use in his lamp. Another needed some to lubricate a wheel. Since all the requests seemed legitimate, the lighthouse keeper tried to please everyone by granting their requests. Toward the end of the month he noticed the supply of oil was very low. Soon it was gone, and the beacon went out. That night several ships were wrecked and lives were lost. When the authorities investigated, the man was very repentant. To his excuses and pleading their reply was: "You were given oil for one purpose—to keep that light burning!"

Exploring and embracing our uniqueness is also a journey that philosophical and religious thinkers realize as well. Martin Buber was once quoted as saying, "The Rabbi Zusya said a short time before his death, 'In the world to come, I shall not be asked, 'Why were you not Moses?' Instead, I shall be asked, 'Why were you not Zusya?'" Krishnamurti similarly admonishes, "As long as you are trying to be something other than you are, your mind wears itself out."

From a psychological standpoint, a significant turning point in a mentoring, coaching, counseling, or self-awareness process arrives when the individual is able to grasp the following, simple, seemingly paradoxical reality:

> When we truly accept our limits, the opportunity for personal growth and development is almost limitless.

Prior to achieving this insight, energy is wasted on running away from the self, or running to another image of self. We fear being ourselves and lack the necessary trust in ourselves for personal evolution to take place. Therefore, running in confusion, we fail to take the special place in community that creation has destined for us. This is not about "performance" on our part.

In her autobiography, poet Maya Angelou writes, "A bird doesn't sing because it has an answer; it sings because it has a song." Or, in the words of the ground-breaking psychologist, Abraham Maslow, "A musician must make music, an artist must paint, a poet must write, if he is to be ultimately at peace with himself. What one can be, one must be." When we are in tune with our own sense of self and not driven by egotistical ideas, our central signature strength can be truly *our* gift to others.

A woman who had a miscarriage in the final trimester of her pregnancy taught me the importance of the uniqueness of every human being. When I asked her how she felt about losing her baby, she indicated that she was naturally quite sad about it, but there was one specific thing that particularly upset her:

> When I think of the son or daughter I lost, the one point
> which tears me apart the most is that I shall never know who
> my child was . . . what he or she was like. Would he have been
> a hyperactive boy? Would she have been a pensive girl? I'll
> never know, and that is a special sadness for me.

We who do live, who have been born, and who have a personality that can be known by us and shared with others have a duty to encourage it to evolve. If we don't seek to let our sense of self grow within us but instead abort our talents, we mock creation and our singular place in it. In fact, the community is significantly lessened by our absence. So, given this, the obvious question is "How do we find this central gift so we can feed and enhance it?"

To begin the search for our main signature strength, we can turn to a number of resources to determine what our gifts are and the one theme or word that would best summarize or stand above the other talents for us. Such resources or ways to discover this information include the following:

- Reflecting on the sense we have of ourselves and what we feel we bring to the world
- Taking the simple and practical step of listing our strengths and looking for a common thread running through them (maybe you feel your friends like you because you are passionate, a good listener, gentle, funny, encouraging, loyal, or for some other reason)
- Asking a mentor, senior colleague, therapist, or supervisor you trust and who is familiar with both your life and personality
- Questioning a broader group of friends, family, and colleagues about what they think represents your gifts and the one theme or word that best summarizes your sense of presence to them

Once a choice is made, then reflecting on it further and sharing it with others to see their reaction is a natural next step. This approach helps to see if the theme is the most appropriate or needs to be changed. In my own case, "enthusiasm" seemed to be what my "name" or major gift was. However, after a period of time and discussion with others close to me, I felt "passion" would be a better choice. It was both richer and deeper.

Making the choice is only a beginning of the process. Our goal then is to seek to develop this gift, share it with others in the best way we know possible, and to see how we can truly understand it ourselves. In doing this, we are taking the first major step to determine our own way of living, so we can allow our life to flow in a way that feels so extraordinarily natural that the creative energy, formerly sapped off in defensiveness or trying to be who others felt we should be, now becomes available to us. This allows us, in turn, to be available to others in our professional and personal lives in ways not before possible. We will also recognize that when we step away from this sense of identity and presence, we can get ourselves into a lot of difficult situations. As Zen master, Shunryu Suzuki notes simply and powerfully, "Most problems we create, arise because we don't [fully] know ourselves."

Although this sounds easy, part of the problem is to embark on self-awareness without getting too wrapped up in ourselves. Yet, when we know ourselves and appreciate our own sense of ordinariness, there is a simplicity to living that allows us to move through life without feeling we constantly need to put masks on for those we meet. It sets us up for the next journey that normally occurs starting in young adulthood: *fathoming*.

FATHOMING SELF
(MORE COMPLETELY)

When my path crossed with a friend of mine who had just been chosen to be the publisher of a fine house, I congratulated him on his good fortune and accomplishment. In response, he seemed quite pleased with achieving this level in the publishing world. Yet as he spoke about the challenges that lay before him in his new position, I noticed there was a certain level of apprehension in his voice, so I asked him about it. His response was that he felt that the very reason he got the position would also be the very cause for the difficulties he would have in moving forward as he knew he must in this role at a precarious time in the firm's history.

Since I knew him well, I could see what he meant. He was very talented and had great experience to offer. However, it was his engaging personality that was certainly a significant factor in his being able to land the position. Because of it, he was well liked not only in the company in which he was working but also throughout the publishing field. Now that he was to take a position where he would be in charge, he would need to make tough decisions that certainly would meet with some disapproval and possible anger. Being someone who enjoyed being liked, this would require a change in style or, more accurately, the fathoming of a richer narrative.

In my own case, a similar insight occurred to me as I moved toward middle adulthood. It wasn't caused by a change in roles or a promotion but a more subtle sense that the center of my personality needed more balance. I recognized that the passion that I had been known for, and congratulated on, could be overwhelming or intrusive at times. In addition, when feeling inadequate, an egoistical way to build myself up was by being exhibitionistic rather than passionate. I could see that my passion needed to be pruned but at first was unclear how to accomplish this. After some reflection and discussion with those I trusted, two inner paths or psychological portals became evident to me.

First, I needed to be less assertive in the development of the central *charism* of passion but instead must psychologically "lean back" by taking time for reflection on what was going on and how to proceed. In doing this, after a time it became clearer to me that the bookend to my passion would be "gentleness." This trait would tone down my passion, encourage a better pacing of my interaction with others, and modulate my intensity.

The second path was to appreciate something unexpected. In providing a place for gentleness, a concomitant opportunity that presented itself was that this very trait turned out to be a portal to discovering or exploring further a number of signature strengths that were quietly sitting unexamined and underused within my psychological repertoire. Bringing gentleness more to the center of my approach to life led me to see a more profound role for a new type of listening, for example. This was not simply the case with respect to others as I found myself opening up to self-examination in a less judgmental way. And so, appreciating a "psychological bookend" to my central gift provided more interpersonal room for others to take their place in discussion and actions with me, because they felt my attitude was more welcoming. In addition, it provided an opening for me to look in a more gentle, clear way both at my own faults *and* gifts. For me, self-awareness and presence to others became more than a process of "repairing" myself and others who turned to me for help. It was so much more . . . and more effective, too!

By reflecting on being a gentle presence, I was reminded as well of a lesson given to me that had remained in my awareness but hadn't fallen fully enough into my overt attitude and actions. It originally was spurred on by feedback given to me by a psychiatrist who was my clinical supervisor when I was a student at Hahnemann Medical College and Hospital.

I had just completed presenting a case of a depressed patient to him, looked up, and waited for his response. He looked at me, nodded his head indicating he had heard what I said, seemed to appreciate my assessment, and from my experience with him, I knew he would call me to go even further in my approach. Then after what seemed a long period of silence (although it was probably only thirty seconds), he said, "I think you really did a wonderful job laying out what is wrong with this patient and the problems he faces going forward if his insight and actions don't change for the better."

After pausing again, to let me fully take in what he had said, he then added with what appeared to me to be a mischievous look on his face, "However, if that is all you are aware of, you will do all of the work in his treatment." There was a look now on *my* face that showed he caught me off guard. Seeing this, he waited for me to respond to what he had said, which I did by simply uttering the word, "Why?" To which he answered, "Because you have only elucidated the man's problems, defenses, and shortcomings. If you stop there, you will do all the work because when the two of you are together, you will be the only healthy person in the room. You must also look at his gifts and strengths. Even his shortcomings are often simply the result of his tripping over his gifts in situations where he becomes anxious or thinks in a distorted manner."

Years after this, in a more research-based and comprehensive way, Martin Seligman and coworkers developed this style of self-appreciation and work with others under the rubric now called "positive psychology." This is not simply sugarcoating things or ignoring negative realities. It is a profound approach that appreciates with the same value the positive as it does the negative. Too often, psychology and society in general have valued the negative more and seen the positive as fluff. We only need to watch television and see how the news is reported to see that society has jumped on the disease bandwagon as well.

And so in order to help others and in arrive at a stronger, more complete sense of self, we need to ask ourselves (as well as others) questions that will open us up. (See Box 7-1.)

A fuller understanding of the primary balancing talent we have (as well as the other less developed ones) enables early to middle adulthood to become richer for us as well as those in our family, circle of friends, and those others who seek our help personally or professionally. Such clarity also helps us avoid being novelists about our lives in which we mix fiction

Box 7.1 Questions to Enhance Self-Exploration and Personal Growth

- In addition to the strength you are known for, what other "lesser" talents do you have that are worth enjoying, developing, and sharing with others at this point?
- How would you foster their increased use with others?
- What new strategies might you employ in facing past obstacles to enhance your personal and professional growth?
- In what way have you found that your own challenges or the suffering of other people have enabled you to deepen and appreciate your life more fully?
- What are some recent experiences or ways of viewing yourself that you felt broadened your sense of self?
- In terms of your own strengths and virtues, what are some illustrations of you at your best as a person or helper?
- In looking over your life, what events have made you value your own life differently and more deeply?
- What ideas and beliefs do you hold now, concerning what makes you and others flourish as human beings? How are they different from ten years ago?
- Given your personal mission or career goals at this point, what are your specific plans to achieve them?
- What do others find most endearing about you? How is this different and possibly broader than ten years ago?
- What would you want included in an article written about you at the end of your life? What do you think most people might miss including in it that is important?

(continued)

Box 7.1 (Continued)

- Which of the following traits do you feel you are being called to develop further at this point in your life?[1]

Dependable

Responsible

Open

Flexible

Welcoming

Trustworthy

Friendly

Hopeful

Understanding

Warm

Mature

Enjoyable to be with

Sympathetic

Empathic

Encouraging

Energetic

A problem-solver

A conflict-resolver

Forgiving

Able to postpone gratification

Self-aware

Consider the greater good

Happy

Enthusiastic

Box 7.1 (Continued)

Willing to listen

Strong

A lifelong learner

Considerate

Romantic

Committed

Confident

Emotionally stable

Industrious

Sociable

Able to form close relationships

Able to set aside time for and value reflection, silence, and solitude

Able to easily share thoughts, feelings, and hopes with others

Able to monitor and regulate my own strong emotions before sharing them

Deal well with ambiguities and surprises

Able to set priorities and then follow them

Know what factors contribute to my overall happiness

Able to laugh at myself

Optimistic

Realistic

[1] Some of this list is adapted from my book *Bounce: Living the Resilient Life* (New York: Oxford University Press, 2009.)

with reality to make our sense of self in our own mind more appealing, fascinating, or abiding. Fathoming all of our gifts, small and large, allows the reality of our *total* self to be enough. In such a position, we are "extra-ordinary" and know this is wondrous in and of itself and that it, in turn, allows us to help others explore their sense of self with a greater sense of intrigue and wonder.

Yet, as enriching, encouraging, and helpful to others as this stage from young to middle adulthood is, there is still one more stage in which activity and focus encompass the remainder of one's life (middle through our entire later adulthood) that is even more mysterious and rewarding: *letting go* or *releasing*.

EIGHT

RELEASING: A LEAP INTO THE DARKNESS

We are usually ready to embark on the third journey, the most mysterious one of all, beginning in our forties or early fifties. It is the most mysterious journey because it is counterintuitive to what we have done for our whole lives. It involves a process or attitude that is at the center of any personal growth process during what has been referred to as "the wisdom years," which is that period of time when we take knowledge and add humility to sense life in a qualitatively different way.

As I look back over forty years of being a psychotherapist, mentor, and clinical supervisor of helping professionals, as well as in my reflection on the guidance I have received, there are questions that I wished I could or would have asked. Surprisingly for me, they are almost all about one thing: *releasing* or what many term "letting go."

Maybe I didn't ask such questions, because in pacing the session, they didn't seem appropriate. Possibly as I walked with persons on a turn in their professional or personal life journey,

I felt the question would ask too much—and maybe that was true at the time. Or in my own life, the questions may not have surfaced because I was afraid of where they might lead. No matter what the reason, the end result was the same: less inner freedom and a failure to fully fathom the amazing paradox of letting go.

When people speak of "releasing" or "letting go," it is often in reference to a specific desire, possession, or relationship. But while jettisoning a particular attachment can be the source of new inner "lightness," releasing is so much more than that, although we shall address that as well. What this attitude or spirit offers can be an almost indescribable gift *if* it is fully understood and becomes the cornerstone of an overall attitude of freedom that is constantly renewed and experienced.

There is a relief when you release your grasp—even of something that may initially have been beneficial or practical. When the timing is right, the movement toward new freedom is wonderful. But, to be honest and realistic, such a freedom is often short-lived. The room swept clean no longer remains that way. The empty space that originally opened up new opportunities for creativity, compassion, wisdom, and the experience of freedom in our lives soon starts to fill up again. It need not be with something bad or addictive, but it fills nonetheless; our lives no longer have the sense of the fresh possibility that they once did.

Unfortunately, the harm this causes is not normally felt for some time. And when it is finally discovered, a sense of self-betrayal or remorse is often experienced. This feeling may even lead us to think, "I am back where I started—or even further back than that!"

Conversely, when there is a sense of openness to nurturing an attitude of releasing or letting go, even when grasping becomes temporarily prevalent again, all is not lost. There is at least a recognition of the fact that our new free space has slowly and quietly become contaminated again. This should not be surprising because habit (or the influences from the past and the society in which one lives) can be very persuasive. Inner freedom is not easy to maintain.

Still the good news is that when we are mindful of the natural tendency to retreat to the familiar, a reservoir of integrity always remains within us that values both honesty and clarity. Paradoxically, this awareness of having been pulled back again is also able to seed an even more intense desire to practice letting go anew—maybe this time with greater wisdom concerning the challenges all of us face.

And so when new idols and fears appear, even though they may be temporarily bowed to, the pilgrimage to experiencing life more directly and fully never totally ceases again. The rewards of avoiding grasping and ego tight-fistedness are experienced more quickly. The loosening of one's psychological grip and being able to smile at the amount of peace and joy during the day is felt. Yes, deeply felt. Then everything becomes easier because the art of releasing is experienced and honored more often—not because it should be, but because it simply makes sense.

For this to happen, however, knowledge, discipline, and commitment to enhance our outlooks and practices with respect to opening ourselves up to life are essential companions. With this reality before us, as a way to dispel any notion of psychological romanticism about the process being easy, automatic, or magical, several "field notes" on letting go or releasing will be explored. They are designed to put the experience of others (both their successes and failures) at our disposal. They also are provided as an encouragement to prepare and/or write one's own reflections. This is done to track the ongoing unfolding of our own lives, because this is a simple but powerful tool for learning from personal experiences and reactions.

The goal of using the information assembled here is to aid in appreciating and recording personal breakthroughs, as well as the occurrence of possibly unnecessary mistakes. In the development of one's own set of field notes on inner freedom, a search is immediately undertaken for what works best—given one's unique background, circumstances, personality style, and current beliefs. By unearthing this information, we can begin to more intentionally enjoy the pilgrimage to greater inner freedom as we make new space for the *experience* of, and relationship with, life. We can also see that attending to flowing, rather than merely drifting, with life is such an intriguing and rewarding daily endeavor, in and of itself. Even when it is difficult and we stumble, we learn from these encounters. There can be an ultimate satisfaction even in failure.

CREATING YOUR OWN
FIELD NOTES

Field or clinical notes are about a person's experiences of what is happening around and within them. They are notations made by social and behavioral scientists about what they have observed in others (as well as themselves) while undertaking research and/or treatment of others. For example, anthropologists have long been known for their written personal observations of cultures. Reading Margaret Mead and, in latter recent times, Colin Turnbull (author of *The Forest People*), enlightens us not only about the people being studied but about the researchers themselves. Formal clinical notes or informal journal entries are similar to this.

They are prepared by psychotherapists and some mentors to record the course of the lives of people who come to them for assistance. They also usually offer assessments of the interventions that were recommended and the resistances to such changes encountered in the process. These findings are relevant. They speak to the helpers of their own human state and psychological situation. Because all of us must face transitions, losses, and the requirement to see things in new ways as we move forward in life, this information is essential not only to others who seek some form of help from us but to ourselves as well.

In my own case, I recall the efforts I made to observe and fathom people's feelings, attitudes, and cognitions (ways of thinking, perceiving, and understanding). I also sought to take note of their actions, psychology, philosophies, and hesitations to act in ways that might lead to greater inner freedom, a more powerful desire to be increasingly compassionate with others, and their openness to the ongoing revelation of offering compassion in new ways. I also know that in preparing my own field and clinical notes (by seeking to put my psychological "fingers" on the pulse of my own feelings and thoughts during the sessions), I could not only find out a great deal about those seeking my help but also about myself because of the type of reactions they elicited from me. Certain people have particular effects on us, so we can begin to see patterns that can teach us a great deal about *ourselves* as well as those with whom we interact.

In seeking to accomplish this, I sought to glean wisdom from the writings of other guides I knew, or had read about, in order to see how their reflections and field notes were driving their own self-understanding. It is especially beneficial if, in our reading and reflection, we use as psychological lenses both a sense of the value of releasing as well as an awareness of what seems to be holding us back from encountering a deeper, richer sense of self.

From both classic wisdom and the findings of contemporary psychology, actual approaches to greater inner freedom are there for the taking. All we need do is look at them more intentionally with such a purpose. By doing this, we can better incorporate helpful attitudes and activities that can have immediate and long-term effects on the amount of freedom we have in our lives.

Preparing our own field notes at the end of the day is simple and only takes a few moments. However, those few moments can be invaluable, particularly at this delicate stage in life, because they will record essential information to track one's emotions and thinking going forward. The first step is simply to sit back and reflect on the peaks, valleys, and plateaus of the day. Once a picture is in one's mind of the objective side (what happened), then it is possible to reflect on one's emotions and what one was thinking, perceiving, and understanding about the events of the day. Such an activity can help us see more clearly the vague perceptions and beliefs that often foster our emotional reactions and conclusions. In this way, you can recognize your philosophy and psychology of life more readily and address or correct it in ways that will free you to live life more intentionally.

Then, when the end of life eventually comes, as it suddenly or slowly surely will, with a spirit of releasing and opening up to new experiences at the heart of our lives, we will know that the moment we are in now is being encountered as completely as possible—almost to the point of astonishing awareness.

Consequently, we will recognize that releasing our grasp, opening up to appreciate ourselves, and acting out of such an honoring of who we are in ever deeper ways . . .

- is both a practice and an attitude;
- involves small daily actions and large decisions;
- can be fed, not distracted, by memories of past joys as well as by possibilities for the future;
- never ends with a final breakthrough but rather is, more accurately, a journey during middle through late adulthood of recognizing and embracing inner freedom;
- manifests itself differently depending upon one's personality;
- is worth the time, effort, and respect we can afford, understanding and incorporating it into our overall outlook and daily experience; and finally,
- is a way of living to help us avoid wasting so much of our short precious lives by postponing fulfillment until something else happens in the future.

Greater inner freedom and actual encounters with others in a more fruitful way can begin *now*, if we are willing to act upon what we decide is relevant for us in reflecting on the following lessons and then putting them into practice in a way that makes sense for us.

What is the specific reward? It is a flexibility, openness to wisdom, and lightness of being that an attitude of letting go and being present can bring to us.

What is the cost? As a beginning, it is time spent in reflection on the ongoing themes in this book, the courage to change based on what is learned, and the discipline necessary not to turn back but to keep our hands on the wheel of our lives, even when it shakes.

Not a bad deal when you think about it.

WHERE DO WE BEGIN?

In order to release, obviously we first need to realize that we are holding onto—in terms of material possessions, our identities, and our ways of interacting with others. Surprisingly, this may not be as easy as it might seem. Finding our emotional centers of gravity can be elusive. For instance, what originally was truly beneficial or rewarding behavior over time may have quietly slipped into being something quite different: *grasping*. In some cases, society may also collude with this change, making it even harder to recognize and address.

Once a famous Buddhist monk recalled such an awakening in his own life. He was staring intently at a beautiful piece of pottery. Just then, his abbot walked by and said as he passed, "Stop committing adultery." The comment and observation by someone wiser and more experienced than he was concerning what was actually taking place in his heart provided new enlightenment for him. He could now see what was actually happening. It obviously had nothing to do with a sexual encounter within or outside of the monastery. It dealt instead with the fact that he had moved from admiration of a beautiful piece of pottery—which is a wonderful attitude—to a desire to possess the vase, something unhelpful to someone committed to inner freedom. Admiration allows us to fully enjoy and then move on. With lust, we become captured by the object, person, or cause. We are caught by it in ways that prevent us from appreciating everything else that is also before us as gift.

If we went to a beautiful garden and were held by only one flower, what a waste it would be. Likewise, if we heard only one instrument during an overture, so much would be missed. The sad thing is that we often do just that with many little and large things in life and don't even know it. We become captured not only by our basic styles of dealing with life but also by what seems new, different, or supposedly perfect until it dawns on us that we have been duped by induced needs or society's salesmanship. Eventually, the new becomes familiar, the different becomes part of the same, and what was deemed perfect is finally unveiled for what or who it truly is.

Thus question we may ask is "Why would we continue to fall for the lure of what doesn't turn out to be truly rewarding when in our hearts we actually know better?" A bombardment of formal and informal advertising has replaced a psychology and philosophy of hope. Instead, an "anxiety of entitlement" and a fear that our needs won't be met unless we are aggressive on our own behalf is promulgated. Once again though, why do we continually fall for it? After all, we are pretty bright and have had some pretty revelatory experiences in our lives, haven't we?

John Berger in his book, *Ways of Seeing*, offers some guidance on this:

> Publicity speaks in the future tense and yet the achievement of this future is endlessly deferred. How then does publicity remain credible—or credible enough to exert the influence it does? It remains credible because truthfulness of publicity is judged, not by the real fulfillment of its promises, but by the relevance of its fantasies to those of the spectator-buyer. Its essential application is not to reality but to daydreams. No two dreams are the same. Some are instantaneous, others prolonged. The dream is always personal to the dreamer. Publicity does not manufacture the dream. All that it does is to propose to each one of us that we are not yet enviable— yet could be.

In *The Wisdom of Heschel*, edited by Ruth Marcus Goodhill, Rabbi Abraham Joshua Heschel, whose books reflect profound understandings of what life can offer when it is lived nobly, writes on the question of "needs" in the following helpful way:

> Needs are looked upon today as if they are holy. . . . Suppression of a desire is considered a sacrilege that must inevitably avenge itself in the form of some mental disorder. . . . He who sets out to employ the realities of life as a means for satisfying his

own desires will soon forfeit his freedom and be degraded to a mere tool. Acquiring things, he becomes enslaved to them; in subduing others, he loses his own soul. We feel jailed in the confinement of personal needs . . . [and]we must be able to say no to ourselves in the name of a higher *yes*. . . . Every human being is a cluster of needs, some of which are indigenous to his nature, while others are induced by advertisement, fashion, envy, or come about as miscarriages of authentic needs. . . . We usually fail to discern between authentic and artificial needs and, misjudging a whim for an aspiration, we are thrown into ugly tensions. Most obsessions are the perpetuation of such misjudgments. In fact, more people die in the epidemics of needs than in the epidemics of disease . . .

In these words, Heschel followed up his famous dictum: "What I look for is not how to gain a firm hold on myself and on life, but primarily how to live a life that would deserve and evoke an eternal Amen."

Heschel obviously appreciates the fact that we must begin to see (1) how we have confined our identities to our perceived needs and (2) where the centers of gravity in our days are. In the process of responding to this call to see these truths, we must ask ourselves the following questions:

- Have I imprisoned my identity within my needs?
- Are these needs really the most important things in my life?
- Are these the areas worthy of my life and ones to which I want to give most of my attention?

The true search for inner freedom is *not* for the romantic or those who fanaticize. It is for those who truly want what is left of their lives to be a real journey in living. In addition, by reflecting on the aspects of the following process, the fuse can be lit to see both how exciting and meaningful letting go can be.

- Attend to the spirit and process of letting go each day.
- Be willing to take risks, be courageous, and unlearn what may have been valid but is now stale.
- Recognize the enchantment and vitality of experimenting with your life and the way you approach people, premises, and desires.
- Incorporate a childlike playful nature and more creative view of the world and yourself rather than being captured by an image of adulthood that is deadening.
- Desire to expand your repertoire as a way of exploring a broader self-narrative rather than confining the voice to what others or society has thus far dictated it to be.
- Have the discipline to pursue a spirit of releasing in all aspects of life.
- Be a lifelong learner by taking practical steps to be open, observe clearly and nonjudgmentally, and absorb the cardinal virtue of psychological sages through the centuries, *humility*.
- Seek friends who encourage and also practice a commitment to inner freedom.
- Choose and emulate a person who models a life based on "letting go" to act as a human compass to follow.

- Retrieve memories of when you felt truly free as though you were flowing with life rather than merely meeting certain dictates.

CHANGING THE MEMORY YOU HAVE OF YOURSELF

For our purposes here, "releasing" involves more than simply letting go of things or attachments to others. Middle through late adulthood is a particularly important period where we must be willing to change the limited memory we have of ourselves. In his book *A Path with Heart*, psychologist and spiritual teacher, Jack Kornfield, shares the following story:

> An older man, a lifetime smoker, was hospitalized with emphysema after a series of small strokes. Sitting beside his bed, his daughter urged him, as she had often done, to give up smoking. He refused and asked her to buy him more cigarettes. He told her, "I'm a smoker in this life, and that's how it is." But several days later he had another small stroke, apparently in one of the memory areas of the brain. Then he stopped smoking for good—but not because he decided to. He simply woke up one morning and forgot that he was a smoker.

To this, Kornfield adds with a sense of simple directness, "We do not have to wait for a stroke to learn to let go . . ." Conversely, when we see that our true identities are being compromised by something, maybe a "psychological or spiritual stroke," that awakens us to the fact that we need not be chained to an identity, a spirit of releasing or letting go is what we do need.

The same can be said of our identities when they are tied to the reputation we have with others. When I read a dialogue between a master and a disciple in the book *One Minute Wisdom* by Anthony de Mello, I recognize how foolish all of us are to be tied to this. In the story, the master's disciples knew that he was quite impervious to what people thought of him so they asked him how he had gained such inner freedom. In response he laughed aloud and said, "Till I was twenty I did not care what people thought of me. After twenty I worried endlessly about what my neighbors thought. Then one day after fifty I suddenly saw that they hardly ever thought of me at all!"

There had to be a decision to let go of one's concern—whether it be reasonable or not—as to what people thought about the change. In a broader sense, we can see that the issue of who is the holder of the rights to our own stories is an important issue to be resolved when addressing letting go and inner freedom. Terry Hershey in his enchanting book, *The Power of Pause*, tells the following story about a girl labeled "difficult" that clearly makes this point:

In the 1930s when Gillian was a child, her teachers considered her learning disabled, one of those students who didn't pay attention or focus, and who could not sit still. ADHD was not yet a diagnosis, so Gillian was labeled "difficult." And her parents were deeply troubled.

A school counselor arranged a meeting with Gillian and her parents to discuss the options. Through the entire meeting, Gillian sat on her hands, stoic, doing her best to act natural and well behaved. At the end, the counselor asked to see Gillian's parents privately, outside the office. Before he left the room, he turned on his radio. Music filled the office. Outside the office door, the counselor asked Gillian's parents to look back inside at their daughter. No longer seated, Gillian now moved about the room with the music—free, untroubled, and blissful.

'You see,' the counselor told the parents, 'your daughter isn't sick. She's a dancer.'

This story could have gone another way. Gillian could have been labeled and medicated. Problem solved.

Instead, she was given the freedom to live from the inside out. The result? A lifetime of dance on stage and in films, and an extensive career as choreographer for such shows as *Cats* and *The Phantom of the Opera*. Difficult little Gillian became the great Gillian Lynne.

BEING OPEN TO CHANGING OUR NARRATIVES

Actress Liv Ullmann once shared the following related, deeply felt sentiment regarding her own narrative:

I am learning that if I just go on accepting the framework
for life that others have given me, if I fail to make my own
choices, the reasons for my life will be missing. I will be
unable to recognize that which I have the power to change.
I refuse to spend my life regretting the things I failed to do.

What Ullman is struggling with is the narrative of her life.
A very creative approach to achieving a healthier, richer sense
of self is with *narrative therapy*. Learning a few things from this
psychological school of thought can certainly aid in supporting
an inner journey to be open to a desire to make all things new
in our lives.

Narrative therapy as a process is associated with the
groundbreaking work of Michael White and David Epston.
They were interested in how people's life stories attributed
to them, but not by them, were problematic. In one of their
key maxims, "the person is not the problem, the problem
is the problem." And the problem is a function of a labeling that overshadows alternative stories of possibility that
people have within themselves but may not be in touch with
at the time.

This is not simply the case in clinical settings but in how
we perceive life, *our* lives, in all settings. This is expressed once
again in the words of educator and author Parker Palmer:

> When we lose track of true self, how can we pick up the trail?
> One way is to seek clues in stories from our younger years,
> years when we lived closer to our birthright gifts. A few years

ago, I found some clues to myself in a time machine of sorts. A friend sent me a tattered copy of my high school newspaper . . . [I said in it] that I would become a naval aviator and then take up a career in advertising.

I was indeed "wearing other people's faces," and I can tell you exactly whose they were. My father worked with a man who had once been a navy pilot. He was Irish, charismatic, romantic, full of the wild blue yonder and a fair share of the blarney and I wanted to be like him. The father of one of my boyhood friends was in advertising, and though I did not yearn to take on his persona, which was too buttoned-down for my taste, I did yearn for the fast car and other large toys that seemed to be the accessories of his selfhood!

These self-prophecies now over forty years old, seem wildly misguided for a person who eventually became a Quaker, a would-be pacifist, a writer, and an activist. Taken literally, they illustrate how early in life we can lose track of who we are. But inspected through the lens of paradox, my desire to become an aviator and an advertiser contain clues to the core of true self that would take many years to emerge: clues, by definition, are coded and must be deciphered . . . From the beginning, our lives lay down clues to selfhood and vocation, though the clues may be hard to decode. But trying to interpret them is profoundly worthwhile—especially when we are in our twenties or thirties or forties, feeling profoundly lost, having wandered, or been dragged, far away from our birthright gifts.

Narrative therapy encourages the very skills that all of us need to have in opening up our perspectives as to who we are, can be, and how we might live each day. And this includes our vocations and long-term goals. There are some skills worth practicing with these goals in mind:

- Listen to our hopes, dreams, and ideas so they are not eclipsed or crushed by the attitudes of culture, family, work, or our own previously limited self-definitions.
- Reflect on those "little" events and experiences that gave and give us joy so they can be given further opportunities for expression.
- Give ourselves a chance to reframe our difficulties in light of possibly unexplored gifts and talents.
- Give ourselves the power to author our own stories, because we—not others—hold the "copyright" to our identity.
- Be sensitive to our self-talk (what we mentally tell ourselves about events, people, and ourselves) in order to pick up interpretations and criticism that is not centered in us but in the outside world's set of values and ethics.
- Open ourselves to an array of stories that color our lives (volunteer work may not be considered "important" because the culture doesn't seem to value unpaid activities, but after exploration, *we* may see the good we are doing and the joy it may be bringing us) but have been underrated.
- Participate in rituals and activities that reinforce and stabilize new, more life-giving identities.

Narrative therapeutic views help us to see more and more of life anew in ways that help our perspectives to become more open to possibility. This is done by isolating assumptions we have about ourselves, examining them, and considering alternative views—especially ones developed by *us* and not merely a mimicking of other authority figures (parents, educators, the predominant culture, therapists . . .) no matter how noble their intentions may be.

As Stephen Madigan, author *Narrative Therapy*, notes:

> From the beginning, a central poststructural tenet of narrative therapy was the idea that we as persons are "multistoried." . . . Simply stated, narrative therapists took up the position that within the context of therapy, there could be numerous interpretations about persons and problems. . . . And the very interpretations of persons and problems that therapists bring forward are mediated through prevailing ideas held by our culture regarding the specifics of who and what these persons and problems are and what they represent (abnormal/normal, good/bad, worthy/unworthy).

Madigan recognized that people generally see themselves in a way that is very much in line with prevailing ideologies and, in the extreme, with prejudices or opinions that have nothing to do with their own values. The goal of narrative therapy is to look at many stories and interpretations in people's lives so they can resist being cast in a way that has possibly held them back. This is exactly what we should wish for ourselves and put into practice by embracing a healthy perspective on life and an openness to new views and necessary change.

Furthermore, the surprises that exploring our own narratives can provide not only open us up to expanding our own self-views and horizons, but also set the stage for undertaking a fuller appreciation of the essential role of the balancing word that was chosen during the fathoming stage of life during young to middle adulthood.

The primary question for this phase is "How can I release my primary gift, identity, or charism and take what I have used to balance myself and make it the primary focus for the rest of my life?" Yet at this stage, the move we must make is much more dramatic than in the past two journeys.

In the first journey, we sought to honor the predominant gift at the center of our personalities by taking assertive steps forward to understand and know how to share it. In the second journey, we were called to lean back psychologically so as to fathom the totality of our personalities by finding a trait to balance our major gifts and to use them as a portal to discovering and emphasizing our less obvious talents or signature strengths. In this phase of life, it is like crossing a psychological chasm in that steps forward or leaning back, won't do. We must leap into the darkness to find the other side of, and new depth in, our personalities, which prompts us to ask ourselves:

Why is true releasing an actual leap into the darkness?
What elements account for such a darkness and where are the points of light within this dark encounter?

Using the example of myself that I originally shared, if passion were my "word" or "name" for my central signature strength, and "gentle" was the word I used to balance and seek other lesser gifts in my repertoire so I could lead and share a "gentle, passionate life" more fully, then in this third journey of my life, my emphasis needs to be more on the gentle aspect. I must seek to bring it into the heart of my attitude and to reflect on how my actions or behavior in general reflect such a theme in my life. Yet when this occurs, "psychological darkness" also occurs in the form of failure, discouragement, and a sense of feeling lost at the very time in our lives when we have passed sixty or so years of age and are told we should have arrived. The wonderful balancing force, however, is that if we don't metaphorically run away from experiencing these apparently negative feelings, we will experience new points of psychological "light" that can lead us to greater inner freedom.

UNDERSTANDING THE SOURCES AND POINTS OF FINDING PSYCHOLOGICAL LIGHT WITHIN THE EMOTIONAL DARKNESS

When we focus our attention on the past and the present with an eye to our lesser gifts (in my case, gentleness), we begin to see how we have failed in the past and are truly failing in the present. If, for instance, you wish to be more assertive at this stage of life, when you're known to yourself and others as someone who is amenable to other persons' wishes first, looking at the past when this was not so might cause pain. This is so because you will see the many times you may have stepped back, and now you realize you shouldn't have done so. Similarly, in my own case, as I seek to gain more clarity on being more gentle now, I can see possibly more starkly than ever before the times in the past when I haven't been gentle. Moreover, in the present as I try to be gentle, it also causes a level of upset and disequilibrium because I can see how unnatural it is for me to be the way I now wish to be and how hard it is to accomplish my goal. In other words, it neither looks nor feels natural.

A danger then at this point is that guilt over past failures and currently unsuccessful changes in my way of being may lead to profound discouragement. This may cause a sense of helplessness that might lead to serious dysfunctional thinking and a feeling that progress is impossible. As French philosopher Alain wrote, "You don't have to be a sorcerer to cast a spell over yourself by saying, 'This is how I am. I can do nothing about it.'"

Of course, it is to be expected that feeling incompetent, discouraged, and a failure at changing our central styles of interaction with others and even our own selves can lead to a sense of confusion about who we are at this point. In his journal *Nine-Headed Dragon River*, naturalist Peter Matthiessen notes that during this very stage, "it is difficult to adjust because I do not know who is adjusting; I am no longer the old person and not yet the new."

Roger Housden echoes this reality in *Ten Poems to Change Your Life*: "A new life requires a death of some kind; otherwise it is nothing new, but rather a shuffling of the same deck. What we die to is an outworn way of being in the world. We experience ourselves differently. We are no longer who we thought we were. But I do not suggest for one moment that it is easy. Nor that there are any guarantees. If you start down a new road, you cannot know where it will take you."

Frustration and confusion at this stage is natural and to be expected. One of my own patients who happened to be a psychologist herself said in an exasperated voice after I gave her some feedback, which I intended as a bridge to the next level for her, "You expect entirely too much mental health!"

Yet I think writer Thomas Merton balances the challenge and a more modulated sense of this stage when he first writes and later balances his initial comments by noting, "What matters is the struggle to make the right adjustment in my own life, and this upsets me because there *is no pattern* for me to follow, and I don't have either the courage or insight . . . in freedom. Hence my fear and my guilt, my indecisions, my hesitations, my back tracking, my attempts to cover myself when wrong, etc. . . . The ordinary answers tend to be confusing and to hide the truth, for which we must struggle in loneliness—but *why in desperation*? This is not necessary." And it isn't.

The challenge in taking the three inner journeys mentioned, particularly the last one, is that we need to be empty. We need to be open and able to let go. The problem for all of us is that we don't realize we are full of things that don't allow us to let go and leave room for the appreciation and embrace of new information and, thus, possibility in our present lives.

Harriet Tubman, one of Maryland's most legendary women, who was admired by presidents and poets and had her image on two postage stamps for her work in leading hundreds of slaves out of bondage on the underground railway, was often praised for her work. In response, instead of smiling, she would say wistfully, "I could have freed thousands more, only they did not know they were slaves."

In the journey of releasing, the goal is to pick up where we are "slaves" to an identity that is no longer sufficient and where we are captives to inner dictates, either because we are not aware of the invisible puppeteers in our lives or we feel we have no choice: "This is how I am. I can do nothing about it."

Kenosis, the emptying of self so we can receive more, says the opposite. It holds that we cannot expect to find out what our futures can be if we are full of ourselves as we are and allow ourselves to remain captured by the narrative we have absorbed from others and our own culture. One of the alluring things about a narrative is that it can give us a sense of security, comfort, and assurance because those around us support it, are used to it, and would be threatened by something different. Yet like taking a ride on a boat in which everyone is having a good time, it still can be drifting in the wrong direction.

"Releasing" recognizes this, as well as the psychological understanding we refer to as "predominance theory" in which we internalize the values and fears of others so that it fills our minds and hearts to the extent that we are not able to see the world afresh through our own eyes. This blocks us seeing our own lives clearly. If we cannot see our own lives clearly, then how do we expect to help others see theirs in a fresh way as well?

Because walking these roads to clarity, unearthing what represents the center of gravity in our lives, and consciously replacing it with what we want to predominate are not easy, some preparation would seem wise. Preparation should certainly include seeking help from sessions with actual mentors or reading the words of "virtual" mentors—not just in passing but with carefully thought-out values in mind as we go forward. In addition, a more useful understanding of "failure" is also important, because most people simply see it as something to be avoided at all cost, and this framing of a lack of success will only unnecessarily deplete the energy of those who wish to experience the personal joy of being committed to what is good.

NINE

THE ELUSIVE VIRTUE

Sometimes you will never know the value
of a moment until it becomes a memory.
—DR. SEUSS

When we are young, we receive messages verbally and more powerfully through modeling on how we should live our lives. Each of us will have different lyrics (events, good fortune, or challenges) in terms of what we will do, who we will marry, and where we choose to live. However, there is a sense in most cultures that there are virtues that make up an ethos as to how all of us should behave in relationship with others.

The most prominent of those virtues is known to everyone but rarely mentioned. It is not highlighted in medicine, psychology, nursing, education, or many of the other helping professions. Although seemingly undervalued in general today, it is a virtue that is at the heart of an attitude of openness. As a matter of fact, even for those of us who sing its praises, it can be elusive. Certainly, as the following story shows, I have found that case to be true with respect to myself.

My daughter, son-in-law, and two grandchildren were sitting around the kitchen table for dinner. Once the meal was done, my daughter looked at her children and asked, "What are you particularly good at doing? In other words, what gifts do you think have been given to you so you can live a rewarding life and can help others, too?"

My granddaughters love this type of question and launched into sharing a pretty full list of what modern positive psychology would call "signature strengths." After hearing this recitation by both of them, my son-in-law finally spoke up and asked, "Well, what about *humility*? Neither of you mentioned that." To which my youngest granddaughter Emily immediately asked, "What's humility?"

My son-in-law is not so young that the Internet is his only source of information, so he said in reply, "Well, get the dictionary and let's look it up."

In response, the youngest scurried to find the dictionary, grabbed hold of it, and handed it to her dad. He found the entry for "humility," read the definition out loud, and then asked, "Well, what person comes to mind when you hear this description?" To which, all three of them immediately responded with great enthusiasm, "Mom-Mom!" referring to my wife. To which my son-in-law then asked, "Well, what about Pop-Pop?" to which they all shook their heads from side to side and said, "No. Not Pop-Pop!"

No matter how much we may value the virtue of humility, it is an elusive one—especially for Pop-Pop! Yet because it is an important personal strength, we must all seek it every day, because it is the very "soil" in which personal maturity and a generative outlook grows. Without it, the call for us to develop and take our place in the world is almost impossible. Despite this reality, however, humility seems in such short supply today.

As we look around the world, we rarely see the face of humility. That is one of the reasons why I suspect that when we encounter true humility (not passivity or playing down our own gifts), we take note. True ordinariness is a tangible wonder, and we experience this for ourselves when we actually encounter the spirit of humility in another person or, without labeling it as such, ourselves. The reason that humility is also at the heart of the psychological or inner journey is, once again, that

> *When you take knowledge and you add humility, you get wisdom. And when that wisdom is added to compassion, you get love, and such love is at the heart of a rewarding life.*

Knowing this is only part of the challenge as humility cannot be sought directly. To do so would paradoxically be an act of pride and egoism. However, this doesn't mean we should do nothing about enhancing "the soil" for humility to grow. For example, some of the ways we can welcome and respect this gift are by doing the following:

- Recognize times when we compare ourselves favorably— or unfavorably, for that matter—with others. When we don't over- or underestimate ourselves, life is much more pleasant. A fruit of humility is the ability to recognize *both* our gifts and growing edges with a sense of equanimity.

- Appreciate how much others have played in our successes, no matter how hard we also may have worked. It is essential to recognize that an achievement is not gained solely through our own efforts and talents.
- Notice when we draw attention to ourselves, our accomplishments, and our possessions as a celebration of gratitude for the numerous gifts received. If we draw attention as a sign of our own superiority, something is amiss.
- Avoid or catch ourselves when we are tempted to use sarcasm or humor at the expense of others. This is yet another step in the right direction.

These are but a number of simple steps to keep us aware of the need to see ourselves and our lives totally, clearly, and gratefully. Humility is certainly the important yet elusive ingredient that makes life so much more tasty and easy to live without a sense of distress. It is also tied to the psychological ability to have sound self-esteem because it helps us avoid the dangers and distortion of overconfidence on the one hand and inordinate self-doubt on the other. Humility clears the lens in which we view ourselves, allows us to enjoy the gifts we have been given, and permits us to share them freely while simultaneously not being concerned about their limits. Instead, we do what we can, enjoy what we have been given, and, let fate take care of the residue.

Humility is especially a key, but often underestimated as well as unexamined, aspect of being a compassionate presence to others. With those in our circle of family and friends who seek our help (and our clients and patients for those of us who are professionals), we seek to help them to be fully themselves ("extra-ordinary"). But because much of the impact of this depends on our *presence* to them, it is truly hard if we as nonprofessional and professional guides don't recognize deep within ourselves that true ordinariness is a tangible wonder and seek it within ourselves as well.

Humility is the ability to fully appreciate our innate gifts and our current "growing edges" in ways that enable us to learn, act, and flow with our lives as never before. Prior to this important passage, we may be drained by defensiveness or wander in our own desert chasing a false image of self that has nothing to do with who we are really meant to be.

Most of us know that at some point we need to go through the gate of humility. That is not the problem. The issue is that we are often unaware of the fact that we have actually stopped being humble and, in the process, have lost our sense of perspective and gratitude. If we are lucky, something wakes us up to this fact, even if rudely. The following anonymously written poem shared with me by a friend illustrates the point quite well:

I had a dream that death
Came the other night,

And Heaven's gate swung wide open.

With kindly grace

An angel ushered me inside;

And there to my astonishment

Stood folks I had known on earth,

And some I had judged

And labeled unfit and of little worth.

Indignant words rose to my lips

But never were set free;

For every face showed stunned surprise,

Not one expected *me*.

With humility, knowledge is transformed into wisdom. Such wisdom then ultimately leads us to open up new space within ourselves where we, as well as others, can experience true freedom and love. Humility allows us to be transparent. It is for this reason that it is so important. So much unnecessary worry and stress can be avoided if we treasure this gift. A dialogue from a collection of classic stories and teachings of the early Christian writers (*Patrologia Latina* and *Patrologia Graeca*) told by the *ammas* (Mothers) and *abbas* (Fathers) of the fourth-century desert in Persia and northern Africa illustrates this. It is told from the vantage point of persons totally dedicated to living a full, meditative life of inner peace, humility, and unselfconscious compassion—a place all of us should seek to be in at some level.

The devil appeared to a Desert Father, in the disguise of an angel of the Lord, and said to him, "I am the angel Gabriel and I have been sent to you."

However, the Father softly responded, "See if you are not being sent to someone else. I certainly do not deserve to have an angel sent to me."

Immediately, the devil disappeared. (author's translation)

This is the kind of natural attitude we need to have if we wish the perspective, peace, and joy that result when we know and value our ordinary, transparent selves without wasting the energy it takes to add or subtract anything from who we really are. Humility is an *essential* ingredient in life because it provides a *kenosis*, an emptying of the self. At its core, humility dramatically opens up beautiful space in our inner life that includes a space for

- simplicity amid the complex demands of both home and office;
- solitude to listen to the message of our quiet spirit lest it be drowned out by the day's noise;
- pacing ourselves while resisting the lure of speed and new technology;
- gratefulness and giftedness in a world filled with a sense of entitlement;
- honesty and clarity rather than spinning the truth to our own advantage;
- real relationships in place of mere manipulation of others;
- restraint instead of instant gratification and aggression;
- doubt and deeper questions rather than filling our selves with false certainty and pat answers;
- reflection so that compassion doesn't lead to undisciplined activism;

- generosity where previously only strident self-interest stood;
- transparency where opaque defensiveness is our normal rule;
- sound self-respect in lieu of inordinate self-doubt or unbridled self-assurance;
- intrigue or curiosity about our actions and motivations so we don't wander down the blind alleys of projection, self-condemnation, or discouragement;
- forgiveness so we don't fall prey to rigidity and self-righteousness;
- what will always be true rather than solely having an interest in what is currently in vogue; and
- the courage needed to be ordinary instead of wasting all of our time chasing after what we believe will make us someone special.

Yes, it is the ability to empty ourselves that creates new inner space in our lives for the surprising and remarkable gifts of humility.

HUMILITY IN SILENCE AND SOLITUDE

Anthony de Mello, an Indian Jesuit priest and psychologist, relates the following classic dialogue between a spiritual master and a novice disciple in his book *One Minute Wisdom*:

"Why is everyone here so happy except me?"

"Because they have learned to see goodness and beauty everywhere."

"Why don't I see goodness and beauty everywhere?"

"Because you cannot see outside of you what you fail to see inside."

When we sit in silence and solitude, we expect a sense of peace. At first, this is what happens. We are so glad that we have entered a space where we are free from the fast pace and tensions of life. However, if we sit long enough, we may eventually get uncomfortable, even anxious. We get ideas. We remember things we must do. We want to get up and write these down, make phone calls, or pick up a book.

If we resist such actions, the next phase of the silent period begins. During this period, we hear the noise that is going on in our belief system. Like a radio turned onto "scan," our minds move from different events—both recent and remote— that have emotional power. Hurts, shame, the silver casket of nostalgia, proud moments, anger, resentment, all come to the surface. Depending on our personality style, we may respond to them with projection, self-condemnation, or discouragement that we are still dealing with these issues and old agendas. This is a crucial point on the road to both humility and a spirit of letting go.

Buddhists would gently suggest that we keep our seats and let the stories of the past move through us, acting as though it were about someone else. No judgment. No excuses. No blame.

Just watch. From a Western religious perspective, Amma Syncletica, a fourth-century desert dweller, would also offer encouragement by putting it this way:

> In the beginning of meditation there is struggle and lots of work . . . But after that, there is indescribable joy. It is just like building a fire: at first it is smoky and your eyes water, but later you get the desired result. Thus we ought to light the divine fire in ourselves with tears and effort. (author's translation)

From a psychological perspective, what happens in the silence is that we are able to create an opportunity for the irrational but as yet undisputed thoughts about ourselves and the world to surface. Such thoughts usually remain in hiding because we don't like them. As soon as they surface, we want to avoid or justify them in some way—even when, maybe especially when, we are alone.

This is unfortunate because they are the front line of deeper irrational beliefs that are crippling us. In therapy, supervision, or spiritual mentoring, we begin to see these irrational beliefs for what they are once we have enough trust to share everything that comes to mind. However, think how wonderful it would be if, in the search for our true selves and the desire to experience the inner space offered by humility, we could also do this *with ourselves* through regular, even brief, periods of silence and solitude.

Lacking opportunities for such "uncoverings" and debrief-ings with ourselves, such thoughts are left to attack us at night and keep us awake. They haunt us when events occur in our lives that make us uncomfortable. They pain us when we feel we have done the wrong thing as counselors with clients or in our personal life with family members and friends, or have been mistreated by others in our professional and personal lives. But such suffering at those times, in those ways, unfortunately doesn't teach us anything of worth. What a waste.

Conversely, if we intentionally make the space for—in Buddhist imagery—those "unruly children" running around in our unconscious asking to be faced, calmed down, and welcomed home, then our silence and solitude can become a classroom where we learn what is driving us—usually in the *wrong* direction. Also as was implied by Syncletica in her previous comment, we will have a chance, once the initial dust of delusion settles, to have a space within us to be freer in life and more open to others.

If we see our growing edges clearly—without excuses, inordinate self-blame, or discouragement (maybe because we have not improved quickly enough for our own liking—after all, we are often being turned to as the "helpers" in our interpersonal circles or even in our roles as professional caregivers!)—then the energy usually employed to defend (or sometimes unwittingly attack ourselves) can be more profitably understood and channeled into learning how we might better enjoy the life we have been given. In addition, our lives, and the way we honestly view them, can provide a clearer path in our counseling and personal relationships as well.

Opening ourselves up to past agendas, distorted thoughts, hurtful ideas, and false beliefs that lurk below the surface, and rise into the vacuum we have created in silence, can teach us much. We just need to give ourselves the space to allow these unexamined memories and perceptions to surface so we can see, examine, and address them with love and understanding. The brilliant founder of the school of individual psychology, Alfred Adler, once pointed out that children are great observers but poor interpreters. The un-worked-through interpretations we also made as children that remain within our unconscious and preconscious are really no different—even though some of us are professional therapists and have probably gone through our own therapy as well as intense clinical supervision. We must meet them and allow them to tell their stories if we are to find the truth. Inner freedom is an ongoing process, not a once-and-for-all accomplishment.

Silence and solitude will help us to delve into the joys and darkness in our inner lives to accomplish this. However, we still cannot find the truth and the freedom of humility by ourselves in quiet meditation, although this is a necessary step in the intriguing process of self-understanding and appreciation. For a fuller self-understanding and appreciation of what humility might mean to us in concrete, practical ways that can be transformative, we will also need direction from the different voices present in our trusted circle of friends who help wake us up, encourage and tease us when we take ourselves too seriously, and inspire us to be all that we can be even though we are where we are at any given point in life.

A true spirit of humility helps us to see our gifts and growing edges with a sense of equanimity. True humility helps us let go of our sense of entitlement, rejoice, and be grateful for all the material and personal gifts we have been given in life—especially the gift of who we are. To have such an experience is not narcissism or pride. It's a sense of pure joy to recognize that we've been given intelligence, a sunrise to see, possibly a good disposition, wonderful friends at different points in life, or whatever or whomever we have in our lives for which to be thankful. True humility allows us to enjoy and lift the bushel basket off our talents for everyone in the world to see. We are able to do this without falling into the trap of being an egomaniac because when we are truly honest about our gifts, we also can simultaneously see our "growing edges" or defensive areas. Our lives become transparent.

In most world spiritualities, there is a wonderful recognition of how we can and should constantly embrace true humility by seeing ourselves directly without a coating of psychological makeup. In essence, we must constantly look at those areas in which we are unfree or defensive. Simultaneously, we must never forget to see and be truly pleased that we are gifted as "helpers" in our interpersonal circle or as professionals to be loving persons capable of true compassion. (The recent literature on positive psychology certainly points to this need to

have a balanced view of ourselves, which includes a clear awareness of our signature strengths.)

After a session of sitting *zazen* (quiet group meditation)
with his disciples, Zen master Shunryu Suzuki put humility's
paradoxical quality of being grateful, yet honest about who we
are, to them in this way. He said, "You are all perfect as you
are." Then, after a short pause, and I suspect with a twinkle
in his eye, he quickly added, "But you could all use a little
improvement."

Deep gratefulness and humility go hand in hand because
the issue of *quantity*—something valued in a consumer society—falls by the wayside. Instead, with a spirit of "all is gift,"
the *quality* of so much more around and in us is appreciated.
Yet that gift might seem insignificant without the humility and
gratefulness to open our eyes and ears to all that we are given
each day.

In his book, *Taking Our Places,* senior *dharma* (Buddhist spiritual) teacher Norman Fischer puts this simply and unselfcon-
sciously in the following experience that he was able to embrace
because of the humility and gratefulness he was experiencing
at that moment: "Last night I went to sleep. I heard an owl. At
that moment I truly didn't need or want anything else for my
life, nor did I have the thought that I did not need nor want
anything. Just, 'hoot, hoot.'"

How often all of us have had "small" but meaningful experiences such as this and let them slip by. Maybe we have sat

inside a warm house wrapped in an oversized sweater when it was a bitterly cold day outside, had a stirring and encouraging conversation with a dear friend, eaten a crisp salad that crunched with each bite, or laughed and had our thoughts twinkle as we read a poem, but still didn't fully recognize these moments for what they were: epiphanies of wonder and awe for which to be grateful.

Sadly, more often than we might be willing to admit, even those of us who are professional therapists don't see the daily joys of our clinical practice and life in this way. Like society in general, negative feelings or a sense of distance from our inner selves are our natural spontaneous responses to life. Contrary to this, a spirit of humble gratitude slows us down to recognize the need to pace our lives differently so we can see ourselves, our lives, and our surroundings in a new way. Yet with space within us and the right attitude or perspective that can arise in the proper use of *alonetime*, we can let go and see that new possibilities can arise in the human psyche no matter how dark things become. Given our frequent exposure to trauma, loss, depression, and other serious life challenges, this is certainly an important lesson to embrace *now* for anyone wishing to be a compassionate presence, especially those of us who serve as professionals and volunteers in the healing and helping arenas.

Hearing the Whispers of a Rewarding Life: A Brief Epilogue

Sometimes our light goes out but is blown into flame by another human being. Each of us owes deepest thanks to those who have rekindled the light.

—Albert Schweitzer, French-German theologian, organist, philosopher, and physician

Sometimes photos of scenes depict a basic principle of compassion and initiative that wakes us up to a simple fact of life we must always remember. One such photo for me was of a scene in a park. In the park, there is a series of bronze statues that have a unique feel to them. At the lead is a woman playing a violin. Following her in line, holding hands are five children, then a space followed by a sixth child reaching out her hand. In the photo of the scene I saw, there was a real child, a little girl, in the picture. In it she has taken up residence in that space and is facing while reaching out and holding the hand of the child left behind.

That is the space those of us who care enter as well. When we do reach out to our families, friends, or others in need, *we* are that child. Yet to be able to continue to enter such spaces left by the needs of others—be we professionals or not—we must be able to remain open. We need to continually seek to learn new facets of what it means to be a compassionate presence and to accomplish this, we must be open to continually learning things anew—not simply about the helping process but about ourselves.

In a cartoon that brought a broad smile to my face, a little girl is pictured with a very official expression on her face, marching into her house after coming from school. Her mother greets her with the question, "Did you learn a lot on your first day at school?" To which her daughter responds, "Yes, but they want me to come back tomorrow anyway."

If most people—especially those of us who are helping or healing professionals—were asked, "Do you really know what is involved in being committed to *remaining* a compassionate presence to others?" the answer would probably be in the affirmative. Yet the facts don't bear this out. Each year many caregivers leave the helping arena. Instead of deepening as people as a result of the important work they are doing, they become burned out, disillusioned, or broken themselves.

In a similar vein, if helpers were asked who is receiving the benefits of the interactions in the therapy room, hospital, school, clinic, or ministerial setting, the almost automatic response would be, "Why the client, patient, student, parishioner, or person seeking help, of course." Yet when compassionate persons we admire are asked the same question, we may hear a different response. Mahatma Gandhi, for instance, when praised for all he had done for India, said, "I didn't do it for India. I did it for myself."

Faithful helpers who thrive—be they professionals or someone caring for a relative or trying to be a good parent or friend—do not merely *endure* the hardships of helping. Instead, their attitude of reaching out to others is based on a recognition that they will deepen themselves as a result of their compassionate efforts. Enjoying the personal fruits of being compassionate toward others is part of hearing the whispers of a rewarding life.

A colleague from Johns Hopkins Hospital shared evidence of this when she returned from Haiti after being there to help following their earthquake. She encountered two events there that woke her up to see life differently through the appreciation of something she had known all along but now comprehended much more deeply.

As a physician, she jumped right in to help immediately after landing in Port au Prince. One of her first tasks was to operate on a little boy who was standing next to a cement wall that crumbled. In the wall was a steel retaining rod that shot out in the process and pierced both his leg and groin. After removing the rod, she immobilized him so that the healing would have a better chance of taking place properly. As she interacted with him, however, she could see he was somewhat hyperactive and would have difficulty lying still. As a way to keep his mind off of this reality, she gave him a job. She told him that he was to watch her "doctor's bag" because it had very expensive equipment in it and she didn't want it to be stolen. He agreed and was very dedicated to his new job. Even when he went to sleep, he would put his arm through the straps so if someone tried to take it, he would wake up.

Finally, after being there for hours, the physician realized she was hungry. Remembering that she had some peanuts she had been given on the plane during the flight in, she pulled out a bag, opened it, and was getting ready to eat them. However, while doing this, she noticed that the little boy assigned to watch her bag was staring at her. In response, she gave him some of the peanuts, but to her surprise, he did not begin eating them immediately even though he was hungry, too. Instead, he divided his peanuts into two even piles and gave half to the girl next to him. She did the same with the boy next to her and so it continued until the child at the end received one peanut.

The next day she needed to perform surgery on another boy who wasn't so lucky: He needed to have one of his legs amputated. After the surgery, to ensure that the medications were at the right level for pain control and to check for signs of possible post-surgical infection, she developed a routine. She would go in every several hours to check on the boy. In entering the large room where he lay alongside other injured children on paper mats on the floor because they had no beds, she would give the thumbs up and if he felt all right, he would return the gesture.

During one of those visits, she went through her usual motions and when the boy responded positively, she thought she might spend a few moments chatting with him. However, as she started to kneel down on the floor next to him, another bus of children, crying and screaming in pain, arrived. In response, the young boy who had had his leg removed looked up and said, "I don't need you. They need you. Go."

Later on, she said she had learned a great deal from these two boys on whom she had performed surgery. When asked what this teachable moment brought her, she responded, "I learned that even when you are in pain, you can think of others. Even when you are suffering, you can recognize that you are part of something greater than yourself."

This physician was able to learn this not only because she was open to see life differently, *her* life differently, but because she was also a person who already valued resilience. She could be in challenging positions where she could not only help but deepen herself as a person in the process. As Karen Reivich and Andrew Shatté note in *The Resilience Factor*, "Everyone needs resilience. More than fifty years of scientific research have powerfully demonstrated that resilience is the key to success at work and satisfaction in life. Where you fall on the resilience curve—your natural reserves of resilience—affects your performance in school and at work, your physical health, your mental health, and the quality of your relationships. It is the basic ingredient to happiness and success."

Resilience includes such skills and approaches as

- a willingness to treat your body respectfully;
- an appreciation of your own dysfunctional thinking and not allowing it—in Alcoholics Anonymous terms—to "rent space in your head";
- the courage to honestly and thoroughly look at your own ways of coping and tendencies to deny, avoid, or minimize negative information about yourself that can lead to change; and
- developing a greater awareness of your own signature strengths, growing edges (those areas which need improvement), toxic emotions, and effective interpersonal skills (the ability to listen even to difficult people, assertiveness, and self-regulation that includes anger management).

When we don't seek to employ and deepen such skills, we run the risk of losing motivation; becoming sarcastic, cynical, and easily irritable and irritating to others; more attuned to the clock rather than the task; and have a greater tendency to "medicate" ourselves with destructive activities and habits.

Yet with the right outlook, great joy can come from reaching out to others—joy and insight into life that would not have been possible had we not reached out in the first place.

In his foreword to an edited work by Peter Schmuck and Kennon Sheldon on positive psychology, Mihaly Csikszentmihalyi notes that

> . . . human beings are not just self-serving entities, but are rewarded also by a holistic principle of motivation. In other

words, our well-being is enhanced when we devote energy to goals that go beyond the momentary and the selfish. We feel happier pursuing short-term goals than no goals at all; when pursing long-term goals rather than short-term ones; when working to better ourselves rather than just having plea-sure; and we feel happier when working for the well-being of another person, group, or larger entity as opposed to just investing effort in self-focused goals. These relationships seem to hold both at the momentary level of experience, and also developmentally, over the life-span—so that persons who devote more time to hierarchically more complex goals are also, on the whole, happier.

Helping others offers us an opportunity to impact people's lives in so many obvious and subtle ways that are in line with what Csikszentmihalyi just described as goals that produce happiness for the helper. These include

- an opportunity to save or improve people's lives;
- receiving the trust and being part of the dramatic ele-ments of peoples' lives not open to many other people or professionals;
- experiencing a sense of potency because of the impact we may have on other peoples' lives;
- being given the opportunity to interact with a wide range of people and emotions in a myriad of situations;
- being in a position to be both intrigued and challenged by the resistance of a problematic pattern (and sometimes the person carrying it!);

- knowing firsthand the benefit of both good organization and creativity in providing sound care—and the challenges that lie in knowing when one takes precedence over the other; and
- appreciating the essential role that our own personalities, mindfulness, and overall psychological health have in being a compassionate presence.

The joys or "job satisfaction" can be so great. However, as in the case of self-compassion, they are not a given. They must be appreciated and attended to in our lives. There is a need to raise our awareness of what the elements in remaining a compassionate force in life are, so that we can turn the tide in favor of progress over the status quo. These may include workload, variety, challenge, balance, positive feedback, mental stimulation, or an array of many factors that determine whether we can continue "the good fight" in our presence to others.

As we have indicated, resilience is not something one can take for granted. In their book for a business audience, *Resilience at Work*, Salvatore Maddi and Deborah Khoshaba note:

Hardiness is a particular pattern of attitudes and skills that helps you to be resilient by surviving and thriving under stress. The attitudes are the 3Cs of commitment, control, and challenge. If you are strong in the 3Cs you believe that, as times get tough, it is best for you to stay involved with people and events around you (commitment) rather than to pull out, to keep trying to influence the outcomes in which you are involved (control) rather than to give up, and to try to discover how you and others can grow through stress (challenge) rather than to bemoan your fate.

Following this approach, Maddi and Khoshaba suggest studying people you know who are high in resilience. To do this, they pose the following five questions as a way of analyzing the approach these types of people have taken to transform stress into something advantageous for themselves:

1. *What stressful circumstances did he or she encounter?* Was the stress acute (disruptive and time limited) or chronic (a mismatch between dreams, desires, and actual experience)? Remember, sometimes an acute stress stirs up chronic stresses.

2. *What problem-solving actions did the person take to decrease the circumstances' stressfulness?* How did he or she do this? Did he or she follow up on opportunities stemming from the stressful situation?

3. *Did the person's coping efforts include getting supportive assistance and encouragement from other people?* Did he or she reach out to others as well in this process, and if so, how?

4. *How did this person talk about the experience?* When reminiscing, observing, planning, or evaluating the stress, did the person associate the experience with his or her life direction, purpose, and meaning? Did the evaluation express new insights about circumstance, life, and self?

5. *How did his or her coping efforts express hardy attitudes?* Can you fit what he or she said or did into commitment, control, and

challenge (thought the problem was important and worth-while enough to solve, tried to influence its outcome, and used the experience to learn and grow from)?

President John F. Kennedy used to tell the following story about one of his favorite authors:

> Frank O'Connor, the Irish author, tells in one of his books how as a boy, he and his friends would make their way across the countryside and when they came to an orchard wall that seemed too high and too doubtful to try, and too difficult to permit their voyage to continue, they would take off their hats and toss them over the wall—and then they had no choice but to follow them!

As in the case of all of us who believe in compassion as well as those professionals entering and continuing in the areas of social work, medicine, counseling and psychother-apy, nursing, ministry, the military, and other helping are-nas, we have already thrown "our hats" over the wall. The information provided in this book is designed to offer some sense of direction with respect to how we can negotiate "the high walls" of being compassionate and so remain firm in our commitment to listen to the whispers of a rewarding life that are present when we continue to be a caring presence to others.

Once again, it is not *if* we will experience darkness in a life well lived. It is *when*. In the case of professional helpers and healers who came in for therapy or mentoring, I found that at about the tenth session, they had built up enough trust to share much of what was bothering them about their situations and, more poignantly, about themselves. And when I would encounter their sadness and rage as their feelings of impotence, experiences of being misunderstood, and stress were tangibly before us, I would, of course, feel to some extent the darkness growing within me as well. In response, I would often think, "If only you realized how good you are. How gentle and assertive you have been in so many situations and what a positive difference you have made in so many lives."

That is the same feeling and thoughts that I wish to extend to you. Because if you are not in darkness now or have not recently been, you will be at some point. Tough periods come for all people who care and are fully involved in life. In response to this darkness, some enter therapy, read self-help books, or reach out to good friends. All of this helps and should be done. However, the darkness often does not lift as fast as we would like.

The lessons of the main section of this book and the "personal retreat" to follow are not presented because it is possible to avoid, lessen, or lift more quickly the necessary darkness that comes with the challenges of life. However, by reflection on the need for self-compassion and how to effectively reach out to others with a sense of openness to what we can be taught, there is a real possibility for profound positive change. Why? Because to be truly open, we experience humility and, once again, when we take humility and add it to knowledge we get wisdom. When we take that very wisdom and add it to compassion, we get love, and such love is at the heart of being a true friend to others . . . actually, it is at the heart of a truly rewarding life.

Reaching Out (and Within) . . . Without Being Pulled Down: A Self-Directed Resiliency Retreat

Is there a quiet stream underneath the fluctuating affirmations and rejections of my little world? Is there a still point where my life is anchored and from which I can reach out with hope and courage and confidence?

—Henri J. M. Nouwen, *The Genesee Diary*

The pessimist complains about the wind;
the optimist expects it to change,
and the realist adjusts the sails.

—William Arthur Ward

When nineteenth-century author Robert Louis Stevenson was a small child in rural Scotland, he lived in a hillside house just outside the local village. At night during the winter months, he would wait until evening was coming and would position himself by the window facing the village below. He would watch carefully for the arrival of the lamplighter who would walk through the village with a torch, setting light to each street lamp. Finally, when he at last caught first glimpse of him he would yell to his mother who was busy preparing dinner in the kitchen, "Look mom! There's the person who pokes holes in the darkness."

Anyone who truly seeks to be compassionate seeks to do just that: poke holes in the darkness of someone else's experience of life so they may see new light in how they view themselves and the situation. Yet, in keeping with the overarching theme of *Night Call*, unless we attend to our own senses of inner peace, resiliency, self-care, and maintenance of a healthy perspective, we can't share what we don't have. Accordingly, taking the reflective space for silence and possibly, solitude, so we can be mindful and renew ourselves during enjoyable and challenging times is essential.

Yet the response to this need is often a dismissive one, especially by busy parents or those who hold professional roles as caregivers: "I wish I had the time. With all that I must do on the job and given the needs at home, it is impossible." Or some even respond, "Get real! Who has the freedom to take a personal retreat?"

Although such comments are understandable, they often miss the mark and are surprisingly impractical. First, denial and avoidance of the personal needs of a caregiver is a recipe for disaster. When healing and helping professionals or as caring individuals in general we avoid taking out quiet time, we set ourselves up for undisciplined activism that leads to unnecessary burnout. In addition, without allowing time for reflection, we also run the risk of acting out certain behaviors that may be unhelpful to ourselves or others—what is often referred to by professionals as "boundary violations."

When we feel vulnerable and overtaxed, the temptation to do inappropriate things under the aegis of "I deserve something for me as well" can result in inappropriate relations with those we serve and serve with. Finally, the question all of us who care must ask ourselves is, "How practical is it to race to my grave—even if it is seemingly in the process of doing good for others?"

The minimal answer is not to merely promise to take long retreats someday (although actually taking one is certainly a sensible step and not a luxury for those of us who have the room to do this). The response is, at a minimum, to take advantage of the crumbs of "alonetime" (being in solitude and reflective when within a group) that are *already* there in our schedules. Once we do this, then we have to decide how to spend that time. First and foremost, we can take the time simply to relax, sit comfortably but preferably up straight, focus on something in front of us, and simply breathe normally and allow the quiet time to envelop us. During this time, possibly repeatedly counting from one to four or reflecting on a word that means something to us ("gentle," "refreshing," "ocean," . . .) will help us relax and center. Thoughts will come to us and like a train, we need to let them go through our minds without either entertaining or trying to avoid them. Such times, even for a few moments, can renew and teach us much.

Secondly, we can take time out to reflect on a theme of renewal and perspective such as the ones that have been discussed in this book. In doing this, a "self-directed resiliency retreat" becomes something both possible and practical because it can be undertaken for a few moments in the morning, while taking a lunchtime walk, or before bedtime. During this brief time, it may provide a nest of knowledge that the "retreatant" can turn into personal wisdom by applying it to her or his own life.

Whether the few moments are taken at the office or during designated time alone at home, the following themes can easily jumpstart a conversation with self or provide the material for discussing the theme with a colleague, friend, or family member.

Reading through all the topics that follow before taking some reflective time out is not necessary and is not in keeping with the purpose of the "retreat." However, if one has a style of preferring to review the entire list before going more slowly through each topic, then that can be a helpful approach as well. No matter what your approach is, the important thing is to take at least a couple of minutes each day to set into motion the discipline of personal renewal time.

To re-emphasize: It is impractical not to do this because taking time for renewal will help increase the quality of care one can give, the enjoyment and appreciation of one's own life—no matter how intense or dark it may be—and provide a deeper understanding that, once again, *it is not the amount of darkness in the world or in one's self that matters . . . it is how one stands in that darkness that makes the essential difference.* As many in the helping and healing fields well know, renewal is at the heart of resilience and compassion.

Now it is your turn: Take a few moments to reflect on the lessons being offered so you can put them into practice in your own way, given your own unique situation. The following practices and questions may represent a challenge to habitual ways of thinking, perceiving, and understanding, so considering them, especially if they elicit a strong reaction, is recommended.

Phil Cousineau relates an interaction in his book, *The Art of Pilgrimage*, that demonstrates how different life can be when we are willing to risk encountering the mysterious, in his case when a newly met friend encourages him to do so. He speaks about transforming travel; I feel it is even more about how— and with what respect—we are traversing our inner lives each day:

> Ahmet's respectful tone of voice sounded like a blessing. By naming my journey a pilgrimage, he had conferred a kind of dignity on it that altered the way I have traveled ever since . . . In the more than twenty years since that journey, I've traveled around the world, marveling both at its seven-times-seven thousand wonders, and at the frustration of fellow travelers I saw at the same sites, whose faces, if not their voices, cried

out like the torch singer, *"Is that all there is?"* . . . If we truly want to know the secret of soulful travel, we need to believe that there is something sacred waiting to be discovered in virtually every journey . . . Always it is a journey of risk and renewal. For a journey without challenge has no meaning; one without purpose has no goal.

Thus take a few minutes for five days—a weekday self-directed retreat—over the next month to read the following brief entries, reflect on each of them, possibly write down some reactions, and then finally put into action in some way what you believe will enable you to transform your day and the rest of your life into a true pilgrimage toward greater self-understanding, self-expression, compassion, and vitality. If it feels a bit much, remember once again, the philosophy at hand: *No comparison with a person or benchmark is necessary; just begin with a sense of intrigue about yourself.* The only goal is to create an atmosphere, "psychological soil" in which to grow your own awareness of how to learn from daily interactions, compassionate efforts . . . life, in general, really. It is your life. Even helping professionals who guide others must remind ourselves that no one can or will do it for us. Also, once again, when we open space for reflection and personal renewal, not only will we benefit ourselves, but others who count on us to be aware and resilient will receive the reward of a quality sense of presence from us as well. Self-compassion and self-renewal go hand in hand with compassion and the renewal of others.

DAY ONE: SAVOR ALONETIME

Almost everything will work again if you
unplug it for a few minutes, including you.
—ANNE LAMOTTE

One of the most gratifying trips I have ever taken was the one to South Africa to speak on resilience. And one of the most enjoyable parts of this journey was during the break between my presentations in Johannesburg and Cape Town to take a brief photographic safari in the Sabi Sands Game Reserve on the edge of Kruger National Park. In the morning, my wife and I joined four others in an open Range Rover for a three-hour trip into thousands of acres of protected area for the animals.

Because it was their winter at the time, it was quite cool and we were wrapped up in blankets with a hot water bottle to warm our hands. As we quickly drove across the open veldt at the start of the journey, I could see the heads of giraffe above some of the trees, be amazed at the quiet that seemed to envelope me, and smile silently at the small herd of agile springbok jumping in the distance. Although our goal was to see lion, elephant, Cape buffalo, rhinos, and hippos (and we did), this early morning experience was worth the trip halfway around the world. There is something about the feel of silence and being enveloped in a quiet wind that takes one's breath away.

Author and literary critic, Doris Grumbach, wrote in her book *Fifty Days of Solitude*, about her time alone in a way that helps us better understand its value:

> There was a reward for [silence and solitude]. The absence of other voices compelled me to listen more intently to the inner one. I became aware that the interior voice, so often before stifled or stilted by what I thought others wanted to hear, or what I considered to be socially acceptable, grew gratifyingly louder, more insistent . . . My intention was to discover what was in there . . . a treasure of fresh insight?

She also realistically added the doubt and hesitation many experience about being alone or quiet for an extended period of time, writing,

> . . . how right Rousseau was about the modern person. Our points of reference are always our neighbors, the people in the village or our city, our acquaintances at school, at games, at work, our close and distant friends, all of whom tell us, with their hundreds of tongues, who we are. . . . Rarely if ever did we think to look within for knowledge of ourselves. Were we afraid? Perhaps, we thought we would find nothing there.

James Joyce describes a character in one of his novels: "Mr. Duffy lived a short distance from his body." This is often an apt description of most of us. Coming home to ourselves is not easy. Not so much because we're afraid of being present to ourselves but because we have forgotten to make time for it. When I was on Capitol Hill to speak to some members of Congress and their chiefs of staff, I brought back with me a comment made by one of the senators. When asked, "What is the greatest challenge to the American Congress today?" his response was, "Not enough time to think." I would add to this, not enough sense to be truly present to the time we already have.

For example, when they go for a walk, most people really don't notice the terrain they are walking through or the breeze that is in the air. They are in a cognitive cocoon, thinking about some event, interaction, need, or achievement. Mindful walking, to the contrary, is quite renewing. It involves being centered and observant without judgment. Many do not realize it, but taking a mindful walk can have a significant impact on the day . . . and life.

Time alone or within ourselves—*alonetime*—needs to be appreciated in the broadest sense (not just in the extreme where someone goes off by him- or herself to an isolated spot) in the living opportunities that present themselves during our current normal daily routines. When alonetime is appreci-ated, explored, and enjoyed in the right way, we can lessen our projections, become easier on ourselves, and decrease our discouragement when immediate gratification or success isn't granted. Instead, we may feel a sense of inner ease and intrigue about the life we can live that is before us *right now* rather than constantly being postponed into some uncertain future. As we can see in the following reflection by Christopher Peterson, the author of *A Primer in Positive Psychology*, life need not, *should not*, be postponed—even for apparently practical reasons:

> Like many academics, I spent my young adult years post-poning many of the small things that I knew would make me happy, including reading novels for pleasure, learning to cook, taking a photography class, and joining a gym. I would do all of these things when I had time—when I fin-ished school, when I was awarded tenure, and so on. I was fortunate enough to realize that I would never have time unless I made the time. And then the rest of my life began.

Consequently, we need to explore silence and solitude to unearth, appreciate, and fathom the value of such spaces in our lives, as a way of insuring that the rest of our lives will be more centered, rich, and renewing. And as was previously emphasized, this will not simply be a wonderful gift to us, but also for those with whom we relate each day, be it only for a few moments or—as in the case of clients—for a single session or an entire therapy.

Spending time in silence, and possibly at times in solitude, can dramatically impact—for good or for bad—the way we live the rest of our lives. Certain fortunate people have some natural sense of this and say they are attracted to these "spaces" whether for a few moments or, on occasion, a few days. We can see this even in little children when they step back from being active with others to go and play with their toys by themselves, regroup, and feel once again a sense of inner ease.

Adults, as well, demonstrate an appreciation for open moments of silence, the opportunity for some solitude and time to withdraw into themselves to regroup and regain a healthy perspective. These free moments can be captured even when flying on a plane, sitting in a group, or walking down a busy city street. They offer a chance to take a breath, center, and allow the process of meaning-making to be examined anew, so we can see if and how our living is congruent with our hopes. There is clearly a desire in many adults to have the space to be comfortable in their own skins, to have an opportunity to sit with themselves peacefully, to take stock, renew, and achieve a sense of inner ease that translates into the ability to have healthier relationships with themselves and others.

Yet *how* we seek and approach the spaces in our days and lives can make all the difference. The process is not the same as in our search for success in the other areas of our lives.

From a developmental standpoint, psychologist Barbara Powell in her book, *Alonetime*, pointed to the longstanding value solitude has for many cultures.

In many societies, voluntary isolation from others is considered necessary for the completion of certain phases of personal growth. Adolescent males entering adulthood in certain tribal cultures are expected to wander alone in the forest, mountains, or desert for as long as several months at a time. During this period the solitary wanderer is instructed to communicate with the [divine], compose a song, or experience a magic dream. Those who return without their dream may be sent back into the mountains and told to return when they are successful.

Recognizing, Honoring, and Appreciating More Fully the Spaces in Daily Life

As in anything valuable for our welfare and, by natural extension, our clients and the persons who are part of our interpersonal communities, time spent in silence, solitude, and some form of formal or informal mindfulness needs to be respected and fully understood if it is to have a positive impact. Otherwise, such spaces in our lives run the risk of being relegated to being no more than useless empty holes within "the real action" of life or simply represent those times when we merely brood about what we may have said to someone or resent what has happened to us yesterday or yesteryear.

Given this, it is essential—*especially* when we are filling family, volunteer, or professional roles as caregivers—to address the questions that will help us to uncover and enhance the spaces in our lives. To accomplish this, questions need to be addressed, such as

- How can time alone and within ourselves become a more fruitful, enlightening, challenging, and renewing place?
- What pitfalls might we encounter?

- How can we meet such perils in ways that actually result in their paradoxically being an advantage to us?

The dynamics of enjoying and benefiting more from the spaces one recognizes or creates may hold some surprises since solitude and reflective time are often taken for granted or seen as needing no introduction. The feeling often is, "What's the big deal about being alone? Anyone can step aside or become reflective when in a group." As psychologists, poets and writers, spiritual figures, and other searchers have recognized, however, there is so much to learn about time in silence, solitude, and mindful presence. This includes

- uncovering the resistances to and reasons for seeking space in our active lives;
- appreciating the expectations we have for time alone and the surprises it can offer us;
- determining how we can make it a priority;
- experiencing how time in silence and solitude can "positively contaminate" the rest of our day;
- knowing the differences between alone and lonely;
- understanding the simplicity that periods of quiet time can foster in our lives; and
- recognizing the conduit free time can be for "unlearning" as well as new learning for us.

Part of the goal of nurturing one's inner life is to provide a panoply of approaches to how silence, solitude, and mindfulness can be viewed from different, possibly surprising angles. Free, quiet moments will never again be seen as being merely the interruptions or stopgaps in a life of activity and function. Instead, very brief informal periods and formal lengthy times when we are physically alone or within ourselves (even when surrounded by others) will be something else, something more, something into which we can enter to alter our whole lives in some very significant ways.

Alonetime already exists throughout much of your day, no matter how hectic your schedule is. Thus one of the first steps in leaning back so we can capture moments of silence, solitude, and reflection is to recognize them. Crumbs of silence and solitude are easily ignored or swept away. This often results in a vision of being at peace and alone as being in the purview of pure fantasy for most of us. Consequently, while we love to read about a hermit's experience, we let the available spaces in our own days lay unnoticed and unfathomed for what they might be.

If anything then, free time needs to be appreciated first for what it is now in our lives—not for what we would like it to be. Just as people would starve if they continued to read extravagant menus or recipes and didn't eat the simple meal before them, so too would the inner life be starved if we didn't actually experience the quiet, solitude, and a chance to explore one's interior terrain that is already available to us but for some reason is presently being left unnoticed and not fully experienced.

Writer Sara Maitland recognized this in her search for deeper and broader silence. She wrote in her book, *A Book of Silence*, "One of the things I discovered at this point was that there were bits and pieces of silence woven into the fabric of each day and I began to try to keep an eye out for them and move into them as swiftly as possible. Some of these moments I had to create for myself . . . but some were just *there*, waiting for me."

When we seek small moments of silence and solitude with a sense of fervor, it is a fallacy to think that in doing this, we are merely settling for less. Instead, we are moving with our present busy realities in seeking the space that is already available, but being left not fully accessed, to breathe, reflect, renew, learn, and relax, just be.

For most of us there are periods in life that are already open. They might include early morning before the rest of the house rises, at the end of the day after everyone turns in for the night, when driving in the car to and from work, when walking to the restroom, the few seconds before answering a ringing cell phone, during a lunchtime walk, while jogging or at the gym, or waiting in a line or in a doctor's or dentist's office. Conversely, it may be an even a longer period of time, such as when one is home alone or during a scheduled day of renewal.

Cancellations or breaks in our schedules are perfect times to take fifteen minutes to do the following:

- Close the office door.
- Sit in a chair or on a cushion.

- Simply count breaths from one to four.
- Gently look a few feet in front of you at an object that inspires you.
- Simply *be* . . . how hard can that be?

During quiet periods before or after meetings, phone calls, or trips to the store or visits to a friend, as well as between each of them, there are other opportunities presented to us for a few moments of silence and solitude. In addition to this, another opportunity can present itself if you (1) leave for work a bit earlier so you are not racing to your place of business, (2) close your door so no one comes to chat, and (3) take a few breaths before the intensity of your workday or time with young children begins. This allows us then to be mindful (alert, present, and open) to the first persons we meet and the day.

When they are recognized and enjoyed, small crumbs of silence and solitude do two things: they help nourish us immediately, and they inspire and call us to seek more and lengthier periods of alonetime. When this happens, we can then see how such periods bring us to life and help us to feel fresher and more open. We will also begin to more deeply appreciate such important realities as *impermanence* and the *fragility of life* so we value what little time we have here in the world and in the process, respect others who also are here on this earth for a short time. This will also help us to see more clearly how often we are "mindless," which need not be the source of self-castigation but, instead, can be turned into places where we can profitably attend to in both our professional and personal lives.

Some Questions to Consider at This Point

Where in your life does quiet time already exist?

In what parts of your life is it realistic to create some new space where you can relax and practice mindful breathing?

Who are the people in your life whom you admire because they are more reflective and relaxed than you are? What are some basic ways to emulate them?

In what ways can you create an environment in your home and office that is conducive to sitting meditation and mindful breathing?

How can you develop a list of triggers to help you be mindful so you don't just run to your grave thinking that once this task is done you will take time? (These reminders can and should include common daily triggers such as the ring of phone, entering your car to drive to work or on an errand, your morning alarm clock, entering the shower, sitting down to a meal, etc.)

How might you create significant time and occasionally a day or longer in which you have nothing on the schedule? (This may require that you leave the house or office because sitting there may remind you of what you still have left unfinished. Remember that whatever needs to be done to create such a leisure space is worth it.)

DAY TWO: REPLENISHING YOURSELF

What if you missed your life like a person misses a plane?
—WALKER PERCY

If there is an apt proverb for the articulated and unspoken demands many people make of those who are caring for others, including professionals such as physicians, nurses, psychotherapists, counselors, and social workers, it surely must be the Yiddish one: "Sleep faster . . . We need the pillows!"

Kenneth Pope and Melba Vasquez, in their book *How to Survive and Thrive as a Therapist*, note some potentially negative consequences when clinicians (and I would add those of us who simply wish to be a compassionate presence to family members or friends) ignore stress and neglect self-care. They include

> **Disrespecting Work:** Therapists who become depleted and discouraged through a lack of self-care may begin trivializing, ridiculing, or becoming overly self-critical about what they do. . . . **Making More Mistakes** . . . Monitoring, acknowledging, accepting responsibility for, and attempting to address the consequences of our mistakes is one of our fundamental responsibilities. . . . But self-neglect can lead to impaired ability to attend to work. . . . We find ourselves scheduling two clients at the same time, forgetting to show up for an appointment, calling a client by the wrong name, misplacing a client's chart, or locking ourselves out of our

own office. . . . **Lacking Energy:** They may wake up tired . . .
fight to stay awake and alert during a session, wonder how
they're ever going to make it through the rest of the work
day. . . . **Using Work to Block Out Unhappiness, Pain, and
Discontent:** More and more clients, projects, and responsi-
bilities are taken on until little if any free time is available
to reflect on our lives, to spend time alone apart from work,
or to become aware of how empty, demoralized, or miserable
we are. . . . **Losing Interest:** We no longer feel the investment
in the work and the connection to our clients. . . . Lack of
self-care can lead to a lack of caring.

Helpers seem so discouraged at times that they don't
even consider—given the culture and their own personal
resources—that there are possible practical approaches to deal
with environmental and intrapersonal sources of stress in mental health and social work settings. Instead, unfortunately, they
just march on. When I had a session with one very competent counselor who was starting to manifest early symptoms
of chronic secondary stress, such as hypersensitivity, increased
daily use of alcohol, and sleep disturbance, I asked him how he
would characterize his own problem. He said, "I may not be
burned out yet." Then, after a brief pause, he smiled slightly
and added, "But I think I'm experiencing at least a 'brown out'!"
Acknowledging his insight, I asked that given the precarious situation he recognized himself in, what type of self-care
protocol did he design and employ for himself to prevent further deterioration of his emotional well-being? In response,

after sighing, he said, "I only wish I had the time for something like that!"

Time, of course, is so limited for most people today—not just clinicians. More and more I am aware of this even in my own life. Shortly after I received my doctorate from Hahnemann Medical College, a physician who had one of the busiest practices in the area came in for an initial psychological assessment. He was having an extramarital affair. Being a new graduate, I remember carefully formulating a Freudian theoretical diagnosis in my mind. If he were to come in to see me now though, I must confess that I think my first unspoken reaction would be to ask, "Where does he get the time?" For those of us who are called upon to fulfill a caring role (and who among us is not in that category?), time is especially precious. In response, we need to schedule our priorities and ensure that what we do is accomplished in the most effective way possible.

The seeds of *secondary* stress (the pressures experienced in reaching out to others in distress) and the seeds of true passionate involvement are actually the *same* seeds. Once again, the question is *not* whether stress will appear and take a toll on those seeking to be compassionate and caring. Instead, it is to what extent we take the essential steps to appreciate, limit, and learn from this very stress to continue—and even deepen—our personal lives and roles as helpers and healers.

There are so many stresses not only in reaching out to others but also in the *personal* lives of those who help others. A difficult marriage, raising adolescents, physical illness, financial pressures, loss of loved ones—sometimes the list seems endless. Complicating these problems further is that the apparent suggested solutions seem to be unrealistic as well.

Denying the dangers posed by secondary stress, as well as resisting a reasonable process of self-knowledge and self-care under the guise that it too is impractical, is an attitude to be avoided at all cost. Given this distinction between a reasonable and unrealistic self-care process, the premise of this book is tied to a significantly different question than the one just posed. It is not "Who has the time to follow this long list of suggestions?" Instead, it is "Who in their right mind would not take the time to ponder the *essentials* of self-knowledge, self-care, and secondary stress (the pressures experienced in reaching out to others)?"

The practical steps to achieving a new perspective and maintaining self-care are actually quite simple although they are not always easy because of our well-entrenched habits and current workloads. However, these two logjams of resistance can be dealt with in incremental ways by reading the brief treatment of secondary stress, self-care, mindfulness, and positive psychology presented in this book with an eye to seeing new possibilities and then acting upon them *in some initial way*. That, in reality, is neither impossible nor unrealistic. Moreover, isn't a sense of openness to new insights and taking initial actions in a healthier direction actually what we expect of others? Why then should we not expect the same of ourselves?

Naturally, what makes up a self-care program varies from person to person and differs according to the stage of life we are in. As Ellen Baker notes in her book, *Caring for Ourselves,*:

> There are many different ways to practice self-care. No one model exists in terms of definition, meaning, significance, or application. Differences between individuals relate to personal history, gender, and personality, and within-individual differences relate to developmental stage, or changing needs. Such differences influence the substance and process of self-care. For one person at a particular stage of life, self-care might involve maintaining a very active schedule and hiring a housekeeper. For another person, or for the same person at a different stage, self-care might involve considerable amounts of quiet, uncommitted personal time and tending one's own home.

Because such a list needs to be tailored, it is helpful to have a large pool of possibilities from which to choose. Listing a number of them here is designed to spur thinking around what could comprise a self-care protocol in your own case. However, there needs to be a sense that the time we spend on self-care is part of the self-respect needed to live a life of true joy rather than a compulsive rat race under the guise that my profession demands constant presence if I am to be seen as someone who takes it seriously. Knowing which elements you might entertain as part of a self-care program and questions to ponder in the overall development of it are both good initial steps in acting upon the need to take responsibility for yourself.

To renew themselves on an ongoing basis, there are basic elements of a self-care protocol that most everyone needs. It really doesn't require too much to take a step back from our work routines to become refreshed and regain perspective. Some of the basic elements might include the following:

- Quiet walks by yourself
- Time and space for meditation
- Spiritual and recreational reading, including the diaries and biographies of others whom you admire
- Some light exercise . . .
- Opportunities to laugh offered by movies, cheerful friends, and so forth
- A hobby, such as gardening
- Phone calls to family and friends who inspire and tease you
- Involvement in projects that renew
- Listening to music you enjoy

The following list offers other simple measures aimed at self-care and renewal:

- Visiting a park or hiking
- Having family or friends over for dinner or evening coffee
- Going to the library or a mega-bookstore to have coffee, a scone, and to peruse the magazines
- Shopping for little things that would be fun to have but not cost a lot
- Taking a bath rather than a quick shower
- Daydreaming

- Forming a "dining club" in which you go out once a month for lunch with a friend or sibling
- Emailing friends
- Listening to a mystery book on tape
- Reading poetry out loud
- Staying in bed later than usual on a day off
- Having a leisurely discussion with your spouse over morning coffee in bed
- Watching an old movie
- Making love with your spouse
- Buying and reading a magazine you have never read before
- Fixing a small garden with bright cheery flowers
- Telephoning someone you haven't spoken to in ages
- Buying and playing some new music by a singer or musician you love
- Taking a short walk before and after work and/or during lunchtime
- Going to a diner and having a cup of tea and a piece of pie
- Going on a weekend retreat at a local spirituality center or a hotel on large grounds so you can take time out to walk, reflect, eat when you want, read as long as you'd like, or just renew yourself
- Arranging to spend a couple of days by yourself in your own home without family or friends present just to lounge around and be alone without a schedule or the needs or agendas of others

- Getting a cheap copybook and journaling each day as a way of unwinding

In their book *Self-Nurture,* which according to their self-stated goal is primarily written for women, but which is filled with good suggestions for anyone concerned about his or her own welfare, Alice Domar and Henry Dreher refer to the time available as a "time pie." They suggest that once we prepare our list, then see how much time we really allot for what we say we are interested in doing for ourselves. They write

> Now compare your list . . . with your time pie. How much time is indicated on the pie for any of the activities listed? Of course, there may be pastimes on your list that you wouldn't do that frequently, like going to a comedy club. But others, like daydreaming or reading, might ideally be part of a typical day. Do these activities show up on our time pie? Many women who follow this exercise discover that there is *no* time on their pie for any of the . . . items. Others count the time spent on purely joyful activity in minutes rather than hours. This can be a shocking revelation, one that motivates some women to radically transform the way they spend their time.

Questions to Ponder in the Development of a Self-Care Program

As was mentioned, time is a precious commodity. How we allot it, what takes precedence, and with whom we spend it all says a great deal about us and the way we live our lives. In the words of the Dalai Lama in his book *The Path to Tranquility*, "It is very wrong for people to feel deeply sad when they lose some money, yet when they waste the precious moments of their lives they do not have the slightest feeling of repentance." Yet, "waste" for all of us, including professional caregivers and clinicians, sometimes means the wrong thing. Many feel that taking leisure time for ourselves is not "time well spent." Instead, this leisure is seen as almost wrong because of all the demands of people experiencing emotional stress; at the very least, it must be earned by long hours of productivity without any rejuvenating break. To counter this, one must first explore the options available to develop a self-care program inventory that is not a nicety of life but a necessary source of constant renewal so that care for others can be done in a quality fashion over an often long period of time.

Once one reviews such a list, how it is used is crucial. At this point, the challenge that presents itself is *how to formulate a self-care program that we are likely to use beneficially and regularly rather than in spurts.* To ensure that an ongoing systematic program is in place, first we must direct a number of questions to ourselves. This is to avoid the dangers of, on the one hand, being unrealistic in developing a program that we won't follow for long or, on the other, of not being creative and expansive enough. Ask yourself the following questions:

- *When someone says, "self-care" what image comes to mind? What are the positive and negative aspects of this image? Where you stand regarding the* importance of developing your own self-care protocol? How realistic is it to develop your own self-care protocol?

- How do you balance your time alone to renew your energy, reflect on your life, and clear your thinking with the time you spend with those who challenge, support, and make you laugh?

- Self-care and self-knowledge go hand in hand. What types of activities (i.e., structured reflection at the end of a day, informal debriefing of yourself during the drive home, journaling, mentoring, therapy, spiritual guidance, reading, etc.) are you involved in which will help you develop a systematic and ongoing analysis of how you are progressing in life?

- What types of exercise (walking, gym workouts, swimming, yoga, etc.) do you enjoy and feel would be realistic for you to be involved in on a regular basis?

- Who in your circle of friends provide you with encouragement, challenge, perspective, laughter, and inspiration? How do you ensure that you have ongoing contact with them?

- The balance between work and leisure, professional time and personal time, varies from person to person. What is the ideal balance for you? What measures have you taken to ensure that this balance is kept?

- As was previously noted, there is a Russian proverb that says "When you live next to the cemetery, you can't cry for everyone who dies." Self-care involves not getting pulled into the dramatic emotions, fears, and anger that pervade healthcare settings. What are the self-care elements that support a healthy sense of detachment?

- How do you prepare for change, which is such a natural part of life?

- What is the best way you can balance between stimulation and time in silence and solitude so you don't have constant stimulation on the one hand or isolation and preoccupation with self on the other?

- *How do you process "unfinished business" (e.g., failure; duplicity experienced in one's friends, family, and colleagues; past negative events; hurts; fears; lost relationships; etc.) in your life so that you have enough energy to deal with the challenges and appreciate the joys in front of you?*
- *What do you number among the stable forces in your life that are anchors for your own sense of well-being and self-care?*
- *In what way do you ensure that your goals are challenging and lofty but not unrealistic and deflating?*
- *What self-care measures do you have to take because of your gender or race that others of a different race or gender don't have to do?*
- *How has your past experience set habits in motion that make self-care a challenge in some ways?*
- *What self-care efforts are more important at this stage of your life than they were at earlier life stages?*
- *What emotional and physical "red flags" are you aware of that indicate that you must take certain self-care steps so as not to burn out, violate boundaries, medicate yourself in unhealthy ways, withdraw when you shouldn't, verbally attack family or friends, or drown yourself in work?*
- *What do you already do in terms of self-care? In each of the following areas, what have you found to be most beneficial: physical health, interactions with a circle of friends, professionally, financially, psychologically, and spiritually?*
- *What is the next effort you need to make in developing your self-care program? How do plan to bring this about?*
- *Are your holidays and vacations appropriately spaced and sufficient for your needs? What is the most renewing way for you to spend this time?*

- *Are you also conscious of the need for "daily holidays," involving a brief tea or coffee break, a short walk, playing with the children in the evening, visiting your friends or parents, practicing a putt in your office or living room, shopping, or casting with a fly rod in a neighborhood field?*

Reflecting on these questions periodically and responding honestly to all of them can improve self-knowledge in ways that aid in burnout prevention. They also can increase sensitivity to how you live your life in a way that enables you to both flourish personally and become more faithful and passionate in how you reach out to others. Once again, the way one moves through the day depends a great deal on personality style. *Burnout is not from the amount of work but how we perceive it and interact with people as we do it.* Some people complain that they are so busy that they don't have time to breathe. Others with the same schedule intensity reflect on how happy they are that they are involved in so many challenging projects.

Some of us love exercise and thrive on it. Others are more sedentary in their existence. All of us, however, want to be physically healthy. Not everyone likes outdoor activities and vacations packed with touring new sites and experiencing adventures in different parts of the country or world. Some of us prefer the backyard, a leisurely walk, an artist's easel, a fishing pole, a good book or a familiar restaurant. However, all of us like to have time away at different points.

The differences among us are many. That is why each self-care program, if it is to be both realistic and effective, is unique in its composition. The important point , however, is that we must have one in place that we use as a guide every day and not use rationalizations and excuses for not doing this. Not to have a personal self-care program is not only courting disaster in terms of both one's personal and professional lives; it is also, at its core, an act of profound disrespect for oneself.

When we have true self-respect that is evidenced by a sound self-care program, it can be transformative for us. But, as has been alluded to elsewhere in this book, the transformation is not just for us but for others as well because one of the greatest gifts we can share with our coworkers and patients is a sense of our own peace and self-respect. However, you can't share what you don't have. It is as simple as that.

We also need to recognize that when we speak about self-care and self-nurturing, we are not referring here to another intense program that just adds more stress to life in the name of reducing it. Once again, as Domar and Dreher note

> True body–nurture absolutely includes physical activity and sound nutrition, but not compulsive exercise and onerous dietary restriction. True body-nurture is also much more than exercise and nutrition. It includes the following actions and ideas:
> - Deep diaphragmatic breathing
> - A regular practice of relaxation
> - Cognitive restructuring of body-punishing thoughts into thoughts of compassion and forgiveness
> - Delight in the sensual and sexual pleasures of the body

- A sane, balanced, non-shame-based relationship with food
- Health-promoting behaviors, such as stopping smoking, alcohol in moderation, and regular visits to the doctor for preventive care
- A profound regard for the sacredness of the body, including all its functions, imperfections, idiosyncrasies, and wonders

Such an overall approach to body-nurture and the other approaches mentioned thus far will clearly benefit us and help us develop an attitude and behaviors that will improve health and increase personal and, in those cases where we are trained helpers, professional well-being.

DAY THREE: DEBRIEFING

The world fears a new experience more than it fears anything.
Because a new experience displaces so many old experiences.
—D. H. LAWRENCE

In 1994 I did a psychological debriefing of some of the relief workers evacuated from Rwanda during its bloody genocide. I interviewed each person and gave all of them an opportunity to tell their stories. As they related the horrors they had experienced, they seemed to be grateful for an opportunity to ventilate. They recounted the details again and again, relating their feelings as well as descriptions of the events that triggered them. Their sense of futility, feelings of guilt, sense of alienation, and experiences with emotional outbursts all came to the fore.

In addition to listening, I gave them handouts on what to possibly expect down the road (problems sleeping, difficulties trusting and relating to others, flashbacks, and the like). As I moved through the process of debriefing and providing information so they could have a frame of reference for understanding their experiences, I thought to myself, "This is going pretty well." Then something happened that shifted my whole experience.

In the course of one of the final interviews, one of the relief workers related stories of how certain members of the Hutu tribe raped and dismembered their Tutsi foes. Soon, I noticed I was holding onto my chair for dear life. I was doing what some young people call "white knuckling it."

After the day's sessions, I did what I usually do at the end of every day. I do a self-debriefing. In doing this, I first look at the psychological topography of the day beginning with the objective: what happened today. Following this, I get in touch with the subjective: my feelings by looking at the peaks and valleys and asking myself a number of simple questions. What made me sad? Overwhelmed me? Sexually aroused me? Made me extremely happy or even confused me? Being brutally honest with myself, I try to put my finger on the pulse of my emotions.

The first thing that struck me on the day when I had the dramatic reaction to one of the Rwandan caregivers who I was assigned to debrief was the tight grip I had on the chair as the session with her progressed. "What was I feeling when I did this? Why did I do this?" Given each of my feelings, I then looked at the cognitions—ways of thinking, perceiving, and understanding—that were underlying and giving impetus to my emotional reactions.

It didn't take me long to realize that their terrible stories had broken through my defenses and temporarily destroyed my normal sense of distance and detachment. I was holding onto the chair because, quite simply, I was frightened to death that if I didn't, I would be pulled into the vortex of darkness myself.

That recognition alone helped lessen the pain and my fearful uneasiness. Thinking about it all so I could "unpack" both my thoughts and feelings also helped prevent the slide into unnecessary darkness and to learn—and thus benefit—from the events of the day.

For therapists and counselors, a daily review or self-debriefing helps them get in touch with the feelings they have had in their treatment sessions. They seek to discover if their intense encounters with the persons they serve triggered distorted thoughts and beliefs. By looking at their own reactions, they not only learn things about themselves but also appreciate the people and situations they encounter in new ways. Such a review would benefit all of us even if we are not in the helping or healing professions. It is both a simple and powerful process to undertake on a daily basis and need not take too much time.

In more detail, the process of a *structured reflection* or *self-debriefing*, which could be modified according to individual needs, includes the following steps:

1. Pick events during the day that stand out.
2. Enter into the event and describe what happened (the objective) and how you feel (the subjective).
3. Avoid the temptation to be discouraged, blame others (projection) or yourself (self-condemnation); instead, see what you can learn from the event about yourself and your vulnerabilities, needs, addictions, fears, anxieties, worries, and desires.

4. Reflect on these insights in light of what you believe (your philosophy, psychology, ethics, and/or spirituality).
5. Decide how these insights should change you personally, interpersonally, and professionally.
6. Alter the way you behave in light of these new insights.

In the Buddhist tradition, Zen roshis teach that feelings, past hurts, shame, questions, and needs will come to the surface during meditation. These can teach us if we are willing to pay attention to and refrain from judging, blaming, indulging in, or rejecting our feelings. Instead, we must be open to learn from these experiences as we would have others learn from us. In his informative work, *A Path with Heart*, Jack Kornfield points out, "Spiritual transformation is a profound process that doesn't happen by accident. We need a repeated discipline, a genuine training, in order to let go of our old habits of mind and to find and sustain a new way of seeing. To mature on the spiritual path we need to commit ourselves in a systematic way."

We all can benefit from these processes—be it a debriefing, structured review of the day, mindfulness routines, or formal meditation. People who wish to live truly aware lives need to take time out during the day or at day's end to quietly sit with their feelings and cognitions in an objective, non-judgmental way. The more we can do this on a regular basis, the more we can avoid unnecessary darkness and live through the unpleasant events of life in a way that provides direction and learning.

Debriefing ourselves also can be enhanced by sharing this process with someone we trust to accompany us on the psychological and, for some, spiritual journey. When we get feedback from those we trust, we will cut down on the distortion and discouragement that arises when we seek to be truly honest and loving with ourselves. The importance of having the patience and determination to go deeper in our lives sometimes can't be seen until someone else, much wiser than we are, helps nudge us along in the self-discovery process. A sensitive guide who was aware of the important role balance plays in exploring our inner lives once told me this story, which nicely illustrates my point:

> As I reflected on a call I felt to metaphorically "Put out into the deep water and lower my nets for a catch," a childhood memory came to mind. My aunt would advise me on how to draw a cup from a fresh pail of milk. The cream and froth would be gathering to the top, and if you put your mug in straight, it either filled with froth (no substance, shallow) or with all the cream (too rich for your system).
>
> Instead she showed me how to bend over and blow gently on the top, about three gentle blows. The froth and cream would glide over to the sides, and I could then put my mug in deep down and draw up milk and angle my cup in such a way to gather just a little cream as well.

Beautiful! But we have to be willing to patiently, gently, blow the froth and to reach into the depth and draw up such a full, balanced catch.

A "full, balanced catch" involves discovering the following:

- What we were *feeling* (affect) at different points in the day
- What we were *thinking* that caused us to feel that way
- What we were *believing* that made us think or come to the conclusions we arrived at

Not to review and learn from our days is foolish. Moreover, if we don't constantly spend time asking ourselves about why we feel, think, and believe what we do, we will ruin the chance to live a freer, more satisfying life; whereas, when we employ ways to enhance openness to change and increasing clarity, we foster both a healthier perspective and a way of greeting each day that results in our discovering more about ourselves and those around us.

Simple exploration of events, feelings, and cognitions (ways of thinking, perceiving, and understanding) can provide a wonderful resource of material for reflection, adjusting dysfunctional thinking, changing our perspectives to more healthy ones, and ultimately producing important changes in both our attitudes and behavior. Some sample questions follow, which are driven by principles from critical thinking, cognitive-behavioral and schema therapy, as well as classic spiritual discernment literature.

Some Questions to Consider as Part of a Debriefing or Structured Review of the Day

When I fail, do I

- *ask myself what I feel most badly about for not succeeding?*
- *catch myself when I am tempted to see everything as a failure instead of this one event?*

- *give myself the alonetime necessary to be upset, understand, and move on?*
- *see how my own ego is preventing me from being open to all the agendas and learning possible?*
- *appreciate what I can learn about myself that would not have been possible had I succeeded?*
- *learn what contributed to this failure both in myself and in the situation surrounding it?*
- *appreciate how to avoid or minimize failures like this in the future without feeling I must totally withdraw from the scene as a way of dealing with this lack of success in this instance?*
- *see the role of unrealistic expectations and how my own thinking may have contributed to my having them?*
- *see how failure and the pacing of efforts in my life are possibly related because I was moving too fast, slow, or precipitously?*
- *acknowledge personal and professional limitations in my life that can be improved?*
- *miss early warning signs that if addressed could have averted this result?*
- *see this as an impetus to initiate new interpersonal approaches to the challenge in question?*
- *truly recognize that failure is part and parcel of involvement and that the more I am involved, statistically, the more I will fail?*

Do I emulate cognitive behavioral and schema therapists, as well as critical thinkers and spiritual discerners, by seeking the wisdom, intellectual power, and healthier perspective that can result from more carefully

- *examining comfortable, but unsatisfying patterns with an eye to practicing a step-by-step approach to undo and replace them?*

- *recognizing my own gifts, growing edges, agendas, negative emotions, attitudes, motivations, beliefs, and ways of thinking, perceiving, and understanding when a feeling or reaction arises?*

- *seeing "the grays" of life rather than simply shunning ambiguities and seeking only so-called right or wrong answers to the questions of life?*

- *entertaining both the possible and probable as I reflect on a challenge, problem, or question?*

- *appreciating (and then enjoying more fully) the positive elements already present in my interpersonal circle?*

- *uncovering when I over-predict worrisome events and challenge them so even small, potentially beautiful encounters in life aren't missed?*

- *appreciating those times when I tend to exaggerate, catastrophize, minimize, "awfulize," or can't see the humor or nuance in events or interpersonal encounters?*

- *dealing with disagreement, rejection, or change?*

- *searching for what I can understand and let go of when I encounter personal, emotional hot-button issues?*

- *picking up "self-talk" that is defeating in nature such as minimizing or disqualifying the positive; if I feel it, it must be true; if I don't succeed at something, then I am a total failure, and so forth?*

- *balancing the way I am looking at an event by exploring alternative possibilities or interpretations?*

- *recognizing an inclination to see negative and self-defeating behaviors as being a "natural" part of my life rather than a schema or belief to be uncovered, challenged, and replaced with a healthier perspective or life pattern?*

Do I seek further clarity in examining something during my daily debriefing by discovering the following:

- *What emotions are elicited by this particular topic, event, or area and what is the thinking behind them?*
- *What mature and immature agendas do and did I have in this interaction?*
- *On what am I basing my conclusions and interpretations regarding this and what might be some other possible ones that I might see now that I have stepped back a bit from the interaction or event?*
- *What makes this challenge a possibly more difficult or emotional one for me?*
- *What might be some other ways to look at this that I haven't yet considered?*
- *Are there additional details or input I could obtain that might help me broaden or deepen my understanding?*
- *Why might I resist changing my opinion on this? (i.e., What consequences or vulnerabilities are in play here?)*
- *What was unexpected and surprising in what I am now examining?*
- *What is the first thing that comes to mind when I think of this topic, event, and/or person and what can this reaction teach me about myself?*
- *Am I giving enough time for reflection and consideration of the issues at hand?*
- *Am I picking up the "voices" of self or other blame, discouragement, and unhelpful labeling of people and events and responding to them so they don't prevent critical thinking?*
- *What factors do parental, family, corporate, religious, and/or other values and notable past events in my life play in preventing me from thinking more openly about this issue?*

- *What would it take for me to replace possible hypersensitivity with a sense of intrigue about these events or occurrences?*
- *How can I use this particular issue as an opportunity for practicing building resilience and strengthening a healthier perspective by (1) leaning back emotionally from the event, (2) reappraising it, and (3) renewing myself through gaining new wisdom through humility and new learning?*
- *Do I see this as an opportunity to increase my sense of intrigue about where I am spending my energy and learn what the emotional centers of gravity are in my life?*
- *Can I find new abilities in asking myself questions; developing logic and abstract reasoning; clarifying my values and collecting as much information as possible in ways that my self-knowledge and enjoyment of all of life (both what is perceived as bad as well as good) is accomplished?*
- *Can I learn innovative approaches to track dysfunctional styles; enhance life-giving activities and approaches; and become fascinated with learning more and more ways to loosen the grasp of ongoing unproductive habits?*
- *Am I open to possibly opposing views to mine, which may balance or enrich my understanding?*
- *Can I see the unfamiliar as well as the familiar in how I understand my actions?*
- *Can I identify where immediate self-interest blinds me to new information that may lead to a broader, healthier perspective for me in the long run?*

DAY FOUR: ATTENDING
TO MINDLESSNESS

Attention to how one can live more mindfully is something that can be learned.

In addition, when we see and embrace mindfulness in an ongoing way, not only do we benefit, but those who we reach out to in life do as well. For example, it allows us to be more perceptive concerning what is present in ourselves and others without judgment (which would distract us from seeing clearly), so we can experience situations more fully. Still, to do this, just as in the case of undertaking a practice of structured mindfulness meditation, we must always view ourselves as beginners, learning anew each day.

To accomplish this in reflecting on our lives or in meditation, we need to approach ourselves with no preconceived notions of what will happen or a "gaining idea" in our minds as to something we wish to achieve. Consequently, recognizing the following types of mindless behavior and attitudes as persons wishing to honor our caregiving roles as well as the need of self-compassion is a good beginning:

- Getting too easily upset—often over the wrong things (failing to be successful even after we have been faithful to doing what we can) and missing what life is offering us in all interactions and events (an opportunity to learn from our reactions and as well as information from outside ourselves)

- Seeing interruptions only as disruptive rather than as informative or possible, unexpected opportunities to see or experience something new and differently
- Possessing habits and rules that continue to sap life's freshness for us
- Spending too much time in the silver casket of nostalgia or rushing through precious moments of our lives under the impression that living this way is "only practical" and temporary, although these "temporaries" can link together to form a lifetime of mindlessness
- Only fantasizing about both "the spirit of simplicity" and "letting go" rather than seeking to instill them in our own lives in real, concrete ways
- Merely promising ourselves that we will adopt a healthier lifestyle (developing a sound self-care protocol we will actually follow) in ways that don't ever translate into the necessary actions we need to take on a continual basis
- Like many of those who turn to us for help of some sort, spending so much of the time in a cognitive cocoon of judgment, worry, preoccupation, resentment, fear, and regret that we miss the chance to *experience* life's daily gifts happening all around us
- Having our time in silence and solitude end up being boring and emotionally flat rather than renewing because we haven't taken the time to learn a few basic lessons in mindfulness
- Ignoring life's simple gifts, such as laughter, a child's smile, or a good conversation, and instead spending our precious

time focusing primarily on increasing such trivial things as fame, power, security, and pleasure

- Not being able to reframe a canceled event we were looking forward to, a brief illness, or a delay in our schedules as being a spontaneous opportunity for renewal and educative alonetime

- Being unable or unwilling to see transitions as valuable as our destinations even though they make up much of our lives

- Not valuing the "ghosts" of our past memories as the teachers of change but instead, merely experiencing them as recollections that serve to pull us down or fill us with regret or resentment

- Failing to appreciate the need for a sense of *intrigue* about ourselves—including both our gifts and growing edges as persons and counselors—while instead having our efforts at self-appreciation overshadowed by (1) projecting faults onto family or friends who we don't see as supportive, (2) inordinate self-blame, or (3) discouragement when we don't succeed as we would like

- Spending too much of our time running away from what we don't like as well as "medicating" ourselves, seeking security, or grasping rather than simply enjoying and being grateful for all that is around us

When we do this, in a spirit of self-discovery and without self-condemnation, we can even have fun looking at our failures. This should be kept in mind as we look at the following questions. If they are approached with a sense of intrigue, the information gathered can be helpful and the process actually enjoyable. It is permitted to have fun when we look at ourselves.

Some Questions to Ask Yourself at This Point

Ask yourself. . .

Are you easily distracted?

Do you find yourself reflecting on the past a good deal and replaying it in your head as if you could change the outcome, even though in your heart you know you can't?

How often during the day are you preoccupied with the future?

Do you find yourself driving, walking, or going through your daily routine on automatic pilot?

If your positive predictions for the day don't come true, does it spoil the event or interaction for you?

Do you stay in your head for much of the day and not enjoy the sensations and experiences you encounter?

Do you avoid looking directly at the realities in your life?

How you look physically?

What are the pains and losses in your life?

How do you think of your own mortality?

What are your ways of responding to the world's need for compassion?

Do you continue to use approaches that you know in your heart no longer make sense?

Do you realize that if you let go of certain habits, styles, and gratifications, you can be happier but still go down the same psychological roads?

Do you build your image of happiness on the theory that "if only___happened, then life would be great"?

Are you mentally with your colleagues, family, and friends; or is your mind elsewhere in most instances?

Are certain "flowers" in your garden of experiences in life so precious that you are ignoring the others?

Do you find yourself recognizing that there are life's joys to experience, but you can't seem to let go of what's holding you back from enjoying them?

Do you spend more time planning and striving than actually enjoying life?

Are you aware of the elements of your life that remain unlived and untapped and have a plan to address them immediately (one of the worst enemies of mindfulness is to believe you still have time, which allows you to postpone your life for "practical" reasons)?

DAY FIVE: FRIENDSHIP
AND JOURNEYS IN LETTING GO

*A neglected child has never known what love and cooperation
can be; he makes up an interpretation of life which does not include
these friendly forces.*
—ALFRED ADLER

All of us go through periods when we feel left by ourselves, without "friendly forces" to help us gain perspective and know we are worthwhile, competent, secure, and (maybe most of all) understood. Margaret Mead, the famous anthropologist once said that "one of the oldest human needs is having someone to wonder where you are when you don't come home at night." Sometimes friendship implodes our sense of "lostness" during a dramatic event in our lives. Certainly this has been shared with me both by my international students and in my travels to support those who have gone through more in their lives than many of us fortunately will never encounter in ours.

Toward the end of the Zimbabwean war of liberation in 1979, when one of my counseling students was six years old, a fierce battle was fought in the student's small village. He was alone with his four-year-old brother. The battle raged for the whole day, and people were scattered all over the village. About half of all the children in his village died, including his close friends. For a day after the battle, he and his brother were unaccounted for and were presumed to have died with the rest.

Later they were found hidden in a house where they had somehow survived the gunfire and aerial bombs that had destroyed much of their village. Children who had taken cover in similar places had perished, but they had made it. My student told me that as a professional counselor looking back on the event, the impression the community made on him even surpassed the horror of the violence. When I asked him about this, he said, "We spent a great deal of time afterward telling the story of our survival. I believe it is this retelling of our stories and the attention of so many people that helped us to integrate and mitigate the trauma. The village provided an environment for mourning those who had died and for healing those who had survived. Communal ritual practices played a very important part in cleansing the land and the people at the end of the war. I learned to have a great respect and admiration for the leaders of these rituals and the people of the village, and this was not the last time they were to come to my rescue."

From this he learned something that people in rural areas seem to teach each other instinctively, which is that the tragedy of one individual or one family is a tragedy for the whole community. This is a lesson that would be worth absorbing for all of us, no matter where we live. South African poet Mzwakhe Mbuli offers these words in his Zulu poem:

An injury to the head,
Is an injury to the whole person,
Is an injury to the whole family,
Is an injury to the compound,
Is an injury to the village,
Is an injury to the kingdom,
Is an injury to the world.

No one who connects with a healthy community is ever bereft of the chance to both give and receive love and *let go* of any destructive forces within us. It may be a friend who helps us to let go of pain that is holding us back. In reflecting on his release from a South African prison, Nelson Mandela surprised people with the following comment: "As I walked out the door toward the gate that would lead to my freedom, I knew if I didn't leave my bitterness and hatred behind, I'd still be in prison."

It may be a "friend" who through her writings helps us see the life before us differently and gives us the direction and courage to change. In her simple and powerful work, *Dakota*, Kathleen Norris notes, "disconnecting from change does not recapture the past, it loses the future." Words matter, and hers and others can represent a friendly force to help us gain new healthy perspectives in order to walk through our "nights" and help others through theirs.

Being open to new perspectives is especially important as we move through different stages and are called to turn natural, unforeseen, and possibly unwanted corners in our lives. Still, as we readily see in others and possibly not so readily in ourselves, it is not easy, because of habits, fears, and past hurtful experiences. Lily Tomlin is once purported to have exclaimed, "Forgiveness means giving up all hope of a better past."

Letting go means catching ourselves in the act of holding on to a reeling or reaction that is not from a good place within ourselves. A psychotherapist once shared with me, "When I find myself being tempted to be small-minded or mean-spirited, I remind myself of the invitation to be magnanimous, where I find my better self." This better self is one that is more open, one that doesn't deny difficulties but also doesn't see things in polarities of right and wrong or good and bad. The better self is able to be receptive to a richer and more nuanced experience of life, and this is certainly a place where friendship can support such an attitude.

As well as having and encouraging openness, our community of friends must be richly gifted. It must

- include opportunities both to give and receive,
- be heterogeneous enough for us not to stagnate, and
- have a balance of voices (prophetic, supportive, humorous, inspirational) so that we can have the different facets of ourselves fed and challenged.

In addition, and possibly of more importance, we must be open to receive the gifts of knowledge that new friends can offer us through the example of their lives and the stories of their encounters. Such information may even come to us from people whom we have been called to guide. Thus we need to be careful not to be so role bound as "helpers" to fail to realize that compassion is really a circle where we can be gifted as well—*if* we have the eyes to see.

When I was leading a workshop in Thailand, I met a missionary who worked in Bangladesh. He had a fascinating background and because of his deeply caring attitude had met many interesting people throughout his life. One of these people was Mother Teresa of Calcutta. One story he told me involved the time she went begging during a famine in the area where she taught in the war-torn Bengal of 1943.

The students were hungry, and there was no money to buy food to feed them. When reaching out to a rich gentleman from the area for help, he spat on her. To this she simply responded, "That was for me. Now what are you going to give me for my girls?" He was so moved by her humility that he not only gave her alms, he also became a lifelong supporter and friend.

Friendship is a place that many of us do not know fully because we have a preconceived notion of what it looks like in advance. Yet when we have a good relationship with ourselves, the notion of friendship widens because of our sense of inner freedom, ordinariness, and appropriate self-esteem. Having a circle of friends, including those who challenge, support, tease, and inspire us, enables us to take on "tasks of inner freedom," such as

- attending to the spirit and process of letting go each day;
- possessing a willingness to take risks, be courageous, and unlearn what may have been valid but is now stale;
- recognizing the enchantment and vitality of experimenting with our lives and the way we approach people, premises, and desires;
- incorporating a childlike playful nature and right brain sense of the world and ourselves rather than being captured by an image of adulthood that is deadening;
- facilitating a desire to expand our repertoire as a way of exploring a broader narrative of ourselves rather than confining our voices to what others or society has thus far dictated it to be;
- having the discipline to pursue a spirit of "letting go" in all aspects of life;
- being lifelong learners by taking practical steps to be open, observe clearly and nonjudgmentally, and absorb the cardinal virtue of spiritual and psychological sages through the centuries: *humility*;
- seeking friends who will encourage and also practice a commitment to inner freedom themselves;
- choosing and emulating a person who models a life based on "letting go" so we have a human compass to follow; and
- retrieving memories of when we felt truly free or in which we were flowing with our lives rather than merely meeting certain dictates.

Once again, to embark on such journeys in letting go, we need the support of healthy friendship. Although we are tempted because sometimes it seems to be more efficient, it is foolish to attempt to go it alone: "If you wish to go fast, go alone. If you wish to go far, go together" (a Cameroonian saying).

Some Questions to Consider at This Point

Consider these questions on friendship:

Do I have people with whom I can simply be myself?

What type of friends do I value most? Why?

What do I feel are the main qualities of friendship?

What types of friends are already in my life?

What friends are no longer alive or present to me now, but who have made a significant, positive impact on my life? Why do I think they have made such an impact?

Among my circle of friends, who are my personal heroes or role models?

Who are the prophets in my life? In other words, who confronts me with the question "To what voices am I responding to in life?"

Who helps me see my relationships, mission in life, and self-image more clearly? How do they accomplish this?

Who encourages me in a genuine way through praise and a nurturing spirit?

Who teases me into gaining a new perspective when I am too preoccupied or tied up in myself?

When and with whom do I play different (prophetic, supportive . . .) roles as a friend? How do people receive such interactions?

A NOTE ON THIS APPENDIX

Material in this appendix has been adapted from my professional books on resilience so that the information would apply to a broad audience. If you are a physician, nurse, psychologist, counselor, social worker, or a person in ministry or the military and wish to read more deeply on one of the topics discussed, see "Reading Further on Resiliency, Self-Care, and Compassion" for a list of my works.

CREDITS AND CITED SOURCES

Albom, M. (1997). *Tuesdays with Morrie.* New York: Doubleday.

Baker, E. (2003). *Caring for ourselves.* Washington, DC: American Psychological Association.

Berger, J. (1977). *Ways of seeing.* New York: Penguin.

Bombeck, E. (1994). *The best of Erma Bombeck.* New York: BBS.

Brazier, D. (1995). *Zen therapy.* Hoboken, NJ: Wiley.

Chadwick, D. (1999). *The crooked cucumber: The life and teaching of Shunryu Suzuki.* New York: Broadway.

Chödrön, P. (1997). *When things fall apart.* Boston: Shambhala.

Cousineau, P. (1998). *The art of pilgrimage.* Berkley, CA: Conari.

Csikszentmihalyi, M. (1990). *Flow.* New York: Harper.

de Mello, A. (1986). *One minute wisdom.* New York: Doubleday.

de Saint-Exupéry, A. (1974). *Night flight.* New York: Mariner.

Dillard, A. (1989). *An American childhood.* New York: Harper and Row.

Dillard, A. (1989). *The writing life.* New York: Harper and Row.

Dillard, A. (2013). *Teaching a stone to talk.* New York: Harper Perennial.

Domar, A., & Dreher, H. (2000). *Self-nurture.* New York: Penguin.

Elie, P. (2003). *The life you save may be your own.* New York: Farrar, Straus and Giroux.

Fischer, N. (2003). *Taking our places.* San Francisco: Harper.

Gateley, E. (n.d.). Healing, nurturing, birthing. *SEDOS Research Seminar,* 3(6-7).

Georgiou, S. T. (2002). *Way of the dreamcatcher.* Ottawa, Canada: Novalis.

Grumbach, D. (1994). *Fifty days of solitude.* Boston: Beacon Press.

Harvey, A. (1983). *Journey in Ladakh.* Boston: Houghton-Mifflin.

Heschel, A. J. (1983). *I asked for wonder.* New York: Crossroad.

Heschel, A. J., & Goodhill, R. M. (Ed.). (1970). *The wisdom of Heschel.* New York: Farrar, Straus and Giroux.

Hershey, T. (2009). *The power of pause.* Chicago: Loyola Press.

Housden, R. (2001). *Ten poems to save your life.* New York: Harmony.

Kingsolver, B. (1994). *High tide in Tucson.* New York: Harper Collins.

Kornfield, J. (2000). *After the ecstasy, the laundry.* New York: Bantam.

Kottler, J. (2016). *On being a therapist* (5th ed.). New York: Oxford University Press.

MacCaig, N. (2009). *The poems of Norman MacCaig.* Edinburgh, Scotland: Berlinn.

Maddi, S. R., & Khoshaba, D. M. (2005). *Resilience at work.* New York: American Management Association.

Madigan, S. (2011). *Narrative therapy.* Washington, DC: American Psychological Association.

Maitland, S. (2008). *A book of silence.* Berkley, CA: Counterpoint.

Markham, P. (2015). *Circling the sun.* New York: Ballantine.

Matthiessen, P. (1986). *Nine-headed dragon river.* Boston: Shambhala.

McGregor, M. (2015). *Pure act.* New York: Fordham.

Merton, T. (1965). *Way of Chuang Tzu.* New York: New Directions.

Norris, K. (1993). *Dakota.* New York: Riverhead.

Nouwen, H. J. M. (1975). *Reaching out.* New York: Doubleday.

Nouwen, H. J. M. (1981). *The Genesee diary.* New York: Image.

Oliver, M. (2004). *New and selected poems* (vol. I). Boston: Beacon.

Palmer, P. (2000). *Let your life speak.* San Francisco: Jossey-Bass.

Percy, W. (1980). *The second coming.* New York: Farrar, Straus and Giroux.

Peterson, C. (2006). *A primer on positive psychology.* New York: Oxford.

Pope, K. S., & Vasquez, M. J. T. (2005). *How to survive and thrive as a therapist.* Washington, DC: American Psychological Association.

Reivich, K., & Shatté, A. (2002). *The resilience factor.* New York: Broadway.

Ricard, M. (2006). *Happiness.* Boston: Little Brown.

Rilke, M. R. (1954). *Letters to a young poet* (M. D. H. Norton, Trans.; rev. ed.) New York: Norton.

Rinpoche, S. (1994). *The Tibetan book of living and dying.* San Francisco: Harper.

Sanders, L. (1983). *The case of Lucy Bending.* New York: Berkley.

Schmuck, P., & Sheldon K. M. (Eds.) 2001. *Life goals and well-being: Towards a positive psychology of human striving.* Seattle: Hogrete & Hubert.

Simmons, P. (2002). *Learning to fall.* New York: Bantam.

Steindl-Rast, D. (1984). *Gratefulness.* Mahwah, NJ: Paulist Press.

Strand, C. (1988). *The wooden bowl.* New York: Hyperion.

Wicks, R. J. (2010). *Bounce: Living the resilient life.* New York: Oxford University Press.

READING FURTHER ON RESILIENCY, SELF-CARE, AND COMPASSION

Books for a General Readership

Brooks, R., & Goldstein, S. (2004). *The power of resilience*. New York: Contemporary Books.

Joseph, S. (2013). *What doesn't kill us: The new psychology of posttraumatic growth*. New York: Basic Books.

Kottler, J. (2014). *Change*. New York: Oxford University Press.

Neff, K. (2011). *Self-compassion*. New York: Morrow.

Reivich, K., & Shatté, A. (2002). *The resilience factor*. New York: Crown.

Wicks, R. J. (2010). *Bounce: Living the resilient life*. New York: Oxford University Press.

Wicks, R. J. (2014). *Perspective: The calm within the storm*. New York: Oxford University Press.

Wicks, R. J. (2010). *Riding the dragon*. Notre Dame, IN: Sorin Books.

Wicks, R. J. (2011). *Streams of contentment*. Notre Dame, IN: Sorin Books.

Physicians and Nurses

Sotile, W. M., & Sotile, M. O. (2002). *The resilient physician*. Chicago, IL: American Medical Association.

Wicks, R. J. (2006). *Overcoming secondary stress in medical and nursing practice*. New York: Oxford University Press.

Psychotherapists, Counselors, Social Workers, and Ministers

Baker, E. (2003). *Caring for ourselves*. Washington, DC: American Psychological Association.

Brazier, D. (1995). *Zen therapy*. Hoboken, NJ: Wiley.

Figley, C. (Ed). (1995). *Compassion fatigue*. New York: Brunner/ Mazel: Taylor and Francis.

Figley, C. (Ed). (2002). *Treating compassion fatigue*. New York: Routledge.

Kottler, J. (1989/2003). *On being a therapist*. San Francisco: Wiley.

Mathieu, F. (2012). *The compassion fatigue workbook*. New York: Routledge.

van Dernoot Lipsky, L., & Burk, C. (2009). *Trauma stewardship*. San Francisco: Berrett-Koehler.

Werdel, M. B., & Wicks, R. J. (2012). *Primer on posttraumatic growth*. Hoboken, NJ: Wiley.

Wicks, R. J. (2008). *The resilient clinician*. New York: Oxford University Press.

Wicks, R. J. (2012). *The inner life of the counselor*. Hoboken, NJ: Wiley.

ABOUT THE AUTHOR

For more than 35 years, Dr. Robert Wicks has been called by individuals and groups experiencing great stress, anxiety, and confusion to speak calm into chaos. Dr. Wicks received his doctorate in psychology from Hahnemann Medical College and Hospital, is Professor Emeritus at Loyola University Maryland, and has taught in universities and professional schools of psychology, medicine, nursing, theology, education, and social work. In 2003, he was the commencement speaker for Wright State School of Medicine in Dayton, Ohio, and in 2005, he was both Visiting Scholar and the commencement speaker at Stritch School of Medicine in Chicago. He also was commencement speaker at and the recipient of honorary doctorates from both Georgian Court University and Caldwell College in New Jersey.

In the past several years, he has spoken on Capitol Hill to members of Congress and their chiefs of staff, at Johns Hopkins School of Medicine, the U.S. Air Force Academy, the Mayo Clinic, the North American Aerospace Defense Command, the Defense Intelligence Agency, at Harvard's Children's Hospital and Harvard Divinity School, Yale School of Nursing, and to members of the North Atlantic Treaty Organization (NATO) Intelligence Fusion Center in England on his major areas of expertise: resilience, self-care, and the prevention of *secondary* stress (the pressures encountered in reaching out to others.) He has also spoken at the Boston Public Library's commemoration of the Boston Marathon bombing; addressed 10,000 educators in the Air Canada Arena in Toronto; was the opening keynote speaker to 1,500 physicians for the American Medical Directors Association; spoken at the Federal Bureau of Investigation (FBI) and New York City Police academies; led a course on resilience in Beirut for relief workers from Aleppo, Syria; and addressed caregivers in China, Vietnam, India, Thailand, Haiti, Northern Ireland, Scotland, Hungary, Guatemala, Malta, New Zealand, Australia, France, England, and South Africa.

In 1994, Dr. Wicks was responsible for the psychological debriefing of relief workers evacuated from Rwanda during the genocide there. In 1993 and again in 2001, he worked in Cambodia. During these visits, his work was with professionals from the English-speaking community who were present to help the Khmer people rebuild their nation following years of terror and torture. In 2006, he also delivered presentations on self-care at the National Naval Medical Center in Bethesda, Maryland, and Walter Reed Army Hospital to those health-care professionals responsible for Iraq and Afghan war veterans evacuated to the United States with multiple amputations and severe head injuries. More recently he addressed U.S. Army healthcare professionals returning from Africa where they were assisting during the Ebola crisis.

Dr. Wicks has published more than 50 books for both professionals and the general public, including the bestselling *Riding the Dragon*. His latest books from Oxford University Press for the general public are *Perspective: The Calm within the Storm* and *Bounce: Living the Resilient Life*. Two of his latest books for professionals include *Overcoming Secondary Stress in Medical and Nursing Practice* and *The Resilient Clinician*. His books have been translated into Chinese, Korean, Indonesian, Polish, and Spanish. In 2006, Dr. Wicks received the first annual Alumni Award for Excellence in Professional Psychology from Widener University and is also the recipient of the Humanitarian of the Year Award from the American Counseling Association's Division on Spirituality, Ethics and Religious Values in Counseling. rwicks@loyola.edu

INDEX